HELPING
YOURSELF
HELP
OTHERS

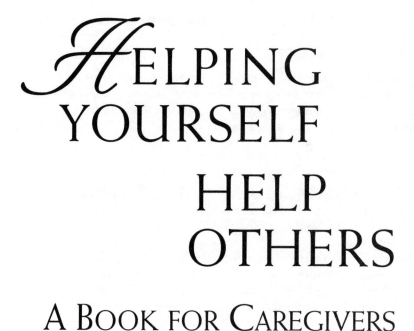

HELPING YOURSELF HELP OTHERS

A BOOK FOR CAREGIVERS

ROSALYNN CARTER

with SUSAN K. GOLANT

RANDOM HOUSE

Grateful acknowledgment is made to the following for permission
to reprint previously published material:

New Directions Publishing Corporation and David Higham Associates Limited:
Two lines from "Do Not Go Gentle Into That Good Night" and
two lines from "And Death Shall Have No Dominion" from *Poems of
Dylan Thomas* by Dylan Thomas. Rights throughout Canada and the
British Commonwealth are controlled by David Higham Associates
Limited, London. Copyright © 1945 by the Trustees for the
Copyrights of Dylan Thomas. Copyright © 1952 by Dylan
Thomas. Reprinted by permission of New Directions Publishing
Corporation and David Higham Associates Limited.

The New York Times: Excerpt from "Keeping the Elderly at Home and
Care Affordable" by Tamar Lewin (February 14, 1994). Copyright ©
1994 by The New York Times Company. Reprinted by permission
of *The New York Times.*

Library of Congress Cataloging-in-Publication Data

Carter, Rosalynn.
    Helping yourself help others: a book for caregivers, 1994.—1st
ed.
    p.   cm.
Includes bibliographical references.
ISBN 0-8129-2370-7
    1. Home care services.   2. Chronically ill—Home care.
3. Chronically ill—Family relationships.   I. Title.
RA645.3.C37   1994
649.8—dc20   94-11924
                                                            CIP

Book design by Charlotte Staub
Manufactured in the United States of America
9   8   7   6   5   4   3   2
First Edition

to my mother

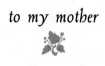

$\mathcal{A}$CKNOWLEDGMENTS

I have written *Helping Yourself Help Others* as a result of a survey done by the Rosalynn Carter Institute (RCI) of Georgia Southwestern College, Americus, Georgia, to determine the needs of those people in our area who provide care for chronically ill or disabled relatives or friends.

I am grateful to Jack Nottingham, the staff of the RCI, and members of the Caregivers Network (CARE-NET) for developing and conducting the survey.

My special thanks go to the students of the college and the family and professional caregivers who participated in the interviews. And I am extremely grateful to those who shared their experiences with me and others at the RCI.

I have included additional information from knowledgeable sources about the issue of caregiving. To all of these people and organizations, I express my appreciation.

Peter Osnos encouraged me to use my personal experiences and those of my mother to further illustrate the challenges and rewards of caregiving. Betsy Rapoport, our editor, was always available with ideas and assistance. I am indebted to these friends at Random House. And Jimmy, my husband, with his patience and advice, helps me in all my endeavors. He gave me valuable suggestions.

My deepest gratitude goes to Susan Golant, my co-author. Without her help with research and writing, this book would not have been possible. She not only worked diligently to gather the needed information from a wide variety of sources, but did so in record-breaking time. I am truly thankful for her fine work.

—Rosalynn Carter

Mrs. Carter's integrity, graciousness, and continuing efforts to help the less fortunate will always serve as models to me. I am also deeply grateful to Irene Pollin, M.S.W., Jack Nottingham, Ph.D., Madeline Edwards, Crystal Williams, my agent Bob Tabian, and Mitch Golant, Ph.D., Mary and Arthur Kleinhandler, and Henriette Kleinhandler.

—Susan K. Golant

ONTENTS

HELPING
YOURSELF
HELP
OTHERS

1.

*W*HAT IS CAREGIVING?

One of my colleagues in the field of caregiving once said, "There are only four kinds of people in this world:

- Those who have been caregivers
- Those who currently are caregivers
- Those who will be caregivers
- Those who will need caregivers"

That pretty much covers all of us!

Family (also called *informal* or *lay*) caregivers are individuals who provide care for chronically ill or disabled relatives or friends. Their contributions can range from less than an hour or two per day to round-the-clock care. They provide services such as grocery shopping; cooking; financial management; errands; housework; transportation; administration of medications, including giving shots, changing dressings, and inserting feeding tubes; personal care such as bathing, shaving, and toileting; and counseling, emotional support, and often just sitting and watching over. They may care for a loved one who is relatively independent but needs a daily compassionate phone call, a loved one who is housebound, or one who is totally bedridden.

My family has had its share of informal caregiving experiences, and more likely than not, so has yours. Indeed, if you have picked up this book, you are probably a caring person. You may prove that every day by actively assisting someone who is elderly or developmentally disabled or who suffers from a physical or mental illness. What a rewarding and noble endeavor it is to help another human being!

Yet I also know from personal experience and from the hundreds of caregivers (especially those caring for mentally ill family members) who have written to me or whom I have encountered before, during, and since my years at the White House that caregiving for those who have been thrust into the role can also be an extremely lonely, stressful, and frustrating responsibility. I have seen so many people who have suffered from having always to take care of another. I know that it can tax one financially, emotionally, and physically. It can disturb privacy, sleep, and even health. Caregivers give so much of themselves and sometimes receive so very little in return.

I have written *Helping Yourself Help Others* to hopefully ease the trauma associated with caregiving and to help you feel not quite so alone. I believe one of the most important missions I can fulfill as a former first lady is to focus attention on you—the family caregiver. You are essential to your loved one's good mental and physical health. I believe you belong to a special category of unsung heroines and heroes who deserve support, services, and praise for your extraordinary personal sacrifices and contributions to our society.

The purpose of this book is to encourage you, to empathize with you, to advocate for your special needs. Perhaps of most importance, its purpose is to give you some ideas, information, and concrete advice that will assist you in carrying out your vital role or in relinquishing it, if the time comes. Of course, I hope this book will help you provide better care, but not only that. I also hope that it will help you have an easier and more enjoyable life.

Before we begin, let me share with you a few general facts about caregiving that may ease your feelings of being alone:

- It has been estimated that only 10 to 20 percent of those requiring care in the United States receive it in institutions. Family members or friends attend to most care recipients at home.
- According to a 1987 survey conducted by the American Association of Retired Persons and the Travelers Companies Foundation, 7 million U.S. households contain caregivers. Perhaps that number is even higher today. Recently, Horace Deets, executive director of the AARP, estimated that there are nearly 25 million caregivers in the United States.
- The National Association of Social Workers has found that 22 percent of family caregivers quit their jobs specifically to give care. It estimates their lost income to be $29,400 per person per year. And caregivers spend an average of eighteen

hours a day giving care—considerably more time than they would spend working at a job.

• "Burnout"—the sense of feeling completely overwhelmed and unrewarded—is common among family caregivers. The caregivers of today who receive inadequate assistance or who cannot share their experiences with others who have the same problems may be the casualties of the future.

• Some family members and friends provide care because of a sense of responsibility and duty, but most do so primarily as an expression of love and devotion to the person needing help.

• Women provide the majority of caregiving in the United States. Sons are usually the caregivers of last resort, and many delegate the job to their wives. Men, when they do engage in caregiving, are more likely to serve as "case managers" than to provide direct helping services.

• The average child who has a chronic physical or mental illness and is being cared for at home requires seventy-one hours of service per week. Compare that to the "normal" forty-hour workweek. Mothers provide the bulk of that assistance.

• The transition into giving or receiving care is often abrupt and rocky. We learn about the caregiving role only when we actually have to take it on. And because of our need for independence, many of us may find it difficult to assume the role of care recipient, even if our lives depend on it.

• Family caregivers face unique challenges: many are called upon twenty-four hours a day, 365 days a year, with few, if any, vacations or weekends away from their responsibilities.

• Caregiving is becoming more and more a part of all of our lives. Because of changes in our society and advances in medicine, most of us can expect to be caregivers and/or recipients for substantial periods of our lives.

In exploring the field of caregiving, I have found that many caregivers have not gotten the recognition they deserve. They may be totally tied down with the burden of someone to care for, yet set aside by society, with their needs, concerns, and problems ignored, even by the medical establishment. It is possible that nobody knows about their situation, that no one cares, or that friends and family simply stay away because they don't know what to say or how to help. It's time for this to change, and I believe this book can be a big step in that direction.

THE INGREDIENTS OF CARING

In 1971, the noted philosopher Milton Mayeroff wrote a slim volume entitled *On Caring*. Although it was published more than twenty years ago, it still has much to teach us about what it means to be a caring individual, and I'd like to share some of the author's thoughts with you.

According to Dr. Mayeroff, caring doesn't mean simply liking someone, wishing that person well, or having an interest in what happens to him or her. (It is possible, for example, to look after another's physical needs without being a "caring" person!) Rather, the kind of caring that gives meaning to one's life consists of helping another person grow and develop. This may be difficult when caring for a loved one who is afflicted with a degenerative disease such as Alzheimer's, but it certainly could apply to the care of a developmentally disabled child or a spouse recovering from the effects of a heart attack or stroke.

Dr. Mayeroff goes on to explain that caring means feeling connected to another, but still appreciating that that person is an individual with separate appetites, needs, and desires. He believes that caring consists of eight ingredients. These are worth exploring here:

1. *Knowing.* We may think of caring as simply having good intentions or regarding someone warmly, but this is not enough. As caregivers, we must know the individuals we're looking after, their strengths and weaknesses. We must also know our own. And we must know how to respond to others' needs.

2. *Alternating Rhythms.* There is a natural ebb and flow in the caregiving relationship. As we care for our loved ones, we learn from our mistakes. We take action and then stand back and evaluate whether we have been effective. Sometimes even doing nothing is the best action we can take.

3. *Patience.* Many professional and family caregivers have told me that learning patience is one of the great rewards of caregiving. When we are patient, we give the individuals cared for time to figure out and do for themselves; we give them space to think and feel. We tolerate the autonomy of the care recipients as well as their confusion and hesitation as they try to move forward. And we must be patient with ourselves. In Dr. Mayeroff's words, when caregivers are patient, they give themselves "a chance to care."

4. *Honesty.* Honesty means being truthful with one's self: seeing loved ones not as one would wish them to be, but as they really are. In so doing, we can better evaluate whether the assis-

tance we're offering helps or hinders growth. But being honest doesn't prevent one from being wrong from time to time. Honesty is a willingness to admit and learn from our mistakes. And it also requires sincerity in the impulse to help. Are we sometimes more concerned about what others will think than we are about seeing and responding to our loved ones' needs?

5. *Trust.* We show a lack of trust when we try to dominate our loved ones or when we become overprotective. Trust means allowing our loved ones to be who they are, to make mistakes and learn from them. Sometimes trust means letting go—allowing others to help in the caregiving. It also means having confidence in ourselves—in our ability to care, our willingness to take risks and learn new skills, our judgment in determining when we must ask others to help out.

6. *Humility.* Humility means admitting that we don't have all the answers—that we must learn more about the caring process. It means that perhaps we can't do it all—we may have to rely on others for assistance. It also means recognizing our limitations and not abusing our power. When we are humble, we acknowledge that we are dependent on others and even on forces over which we have little control.

7. *Hope.* Hope is not wishful thinking or unrealistic expectations about a cure that may never come. It is not arrogance about what can be accomplished. Rather, it is the belief in our ability to take action in the present and the future—the belief that despite our frustrating and challenging situation, we can make a difference in the lives of our loved ones.

8. *Courage.* With the onset of illness in a loved one, we may suddenly find ourselves in new and unfamiliar territory. Everything that was once constant and certain now feels shaky and

ambiguous. Though once we felt sure about life, now we cannot anticipate what the future will bring. Courage is our willingness to come face-to-face with these frightening changes in our lives, to take risks, to attempt to tackle the unknown. We need courage to go forward in our lives at this difficult time.

THE CAREGIVING CAREER

There are many ways to look at the caregiving experience. Dr. Mayeroff's inspiring definition may guide you spiritually during moments when you find your tasks most difficult. But you may also need help in easing the nuts-and-bolts, day-to-day burdens you face with your loved one. You may find comfort in thinking of your caregiving responsibilities as a career that has a beginning, a middle, and an end.

Dr. Carolyn L. Lindgren, an associate professor at Wayne State University College of Nursing, has studied the "Caregiver Career," especially that of those caring for people with Alzheimer's disease. I think we can generalize her findings to apply to all caregivers. Her research explains the stages you might be going through.

THE ENCOUNTER STAGE

This is the moment when you first get the news of your loved one's diagnosis, and it is a time of high stress for everyone. You may struggle to understand what the illness will mean to your loved one, yourself, and your family.

You may suddenly have to deal with hospitals, doctors, treatments, surgery, and a complex maze of professional services with which you are unfamiliar. And as a caregiver you may experience deep personal losses.

Your reaction may be one of shock and disbelief before you can slowly come to terms with reality. Most caregivers also experience a good deal of grief and pain during this period. Unfortunately, you may not receive a lot of support now. Professionals and other family members may be focused on helping your loved one, and you may feel that you can't impose your needs on them. What you need most in this stage is information. You will learn how to educate yourself in your role in Chapter 4.

THE ENDURING STAGE

This next stage is the long-term, hard-work phase of caregiving. You have accepted the diagnosis and are now engaged daily in the potentially grueling job of providing care over months or years.

Depending on your loved one's illness and needs, you may become so engrossed in your caregiving responsibilities that you begin to lose contact with friends and family. It is at this point—especially if your loved one is struggling with a degenerative, debilitating illness—that you might feel hopeless and despairing, frustrated and lost. You might give little thought to yourself or your future. During the enduring stage, however, it's most important for you to set aside time to take care of yourself, especially if the demands of caregiving surpass your resources. I'll have more on how to get the help you need—and especially the benefits of support groups—in Chapters 7 and 8.

The Exit Stage

At this point, your caregiving role diminishes or ends. Happily, your loved one has recovered and no longer needs your care. This is the best of all possible conclusions to a caregiving situation.

But this, of course, does not always happen. It is possible, for example, that your loved one's needs have become too difficult for you to handle at home (even with outside help) or that you will become ill yourself if you continue. In face of the mounting challenge, you may have chosen to place the one you have been caring for in a nursing facility. Your caregiving doesn't end there, however. More likely than not, you will visit as much as possible during his or her institutionalization. You may continue to minister to the emotional needs of your loved one while others look after the physical needs.

Or your caregiving responsibilities may end with the death of your loved one. While many individuals express grief at this time, others experience relief that a difficult period, or their loved one's suffering, is over. Either response—and even both at once—is normal and to be expected. However you react, you must be aware that you might even experience a sense of loss that the activity of caregiving itself has ended. As burdensome as caregiving can be, it also has the potential to lend meaning and purpose to one's life.

HOW THIS BOOK CAN HELP YOU

Of course, we can't always control what happens in our lives—as much as we might want to, none of us can, not even presidents and first ladies. No, we can't control what happens but we can change our way of thinking about it. I hope this book will help you approach caregiving as a blessing as well as a challenging task. I hope that in reading it, you will learn about your own strengths: your patience and hope and courage. I hope that it will help you start thinking about getting help for yourself, perhaps even seeking out a support group. Sometimes knowing how other people cope can help change one's perspective and lighten the load.

In the chapters that follow I will explain how I became involved in this important issue and the research on caregiving that is currently taking place at the Rosalynn Carter Institute at Georgia Southwestern College in Americus, Georgia, my alma mater. I will also explain how to educate yourself and how to prepare for crises as well as the eventuality that you can no longer continue as a caregiver. We will explore together the dilemmas that you must face in this role, the emotions loved ones experience, the changes within your family that may occur as a result of the caregiving situation, and the feelings of isolation and burnout you might encounter.

We will examine ways to cope with your situation so that you can avoid burnout and keep your own health intact. I'll offer some advice on dealing with doctors and the formal caregiving establishment. We'll look at institutionalization as an option and how to make it work. And finally, I'll describe individuals who have found great fulfillment and empowerment in their caregiving roles. For them, caregiving was a difficult burden, but in the end it also brought much gratification.

When Jimmy was president, I had the great good fortune to spend some time with the famed anthropologist Margaret Mead. One of the things I heard her say often was that societies are judged by the way they care for the most vulnerable among them: the poor, the elderly, the mentally ill. It is my hope that you will rise to the difficult challenge of caring for a vulnerable loved one and that you will be able to do so with love, dignity, and courage.

2.
CAREGIVING
IN PLAINS
AND BEYOND

Caregiving has been a familiar part of my life since I was twelve years old. In the spring of 1940, my father became ill. He and my mother had gone on a fishing trip to the Okefenokee Swamp, but they had to come home early because he wasn't feeling well. Once at home, Daddy seemed to be tired and to lie around the house a lot. This was strange to me, since he had always been so strong and active. He used to turn cartwheels and do handstands in the front yard for our entertainment. And he drove the school bus, had a garage for automobiles in Plains, and ran the family farm.

My parents told me not to worry about him, though, and that summer they sent me off to camp for a couple of weeks—my first time away from Plains. I had begged them to allow me to accompany my church friends to camp, to little avail. But in June, they had a sudden change of heart, and I was only too happy to go. I had a great time, feeling only an occasional pang of homesickness and enjoying my newfound independence.

Later, I realized my parents had sent me away and had arranged for my two younger brothers and my sister to stay with our grandparents so that my father could undergo extensive tests at the hospital. The news was bad. He was diagnosed with leukemia.

It was not the custom of the day to inform a patient of the severity of a condition such as this. My mother remembers, though, that as soon as she walked into Daddy's room after learning of the diagnosis and he saw her face, he said, "I want to go home. I don't want to die in the hospital."

And so Mother took him home.

When I returned from camp, the rhythm of our lives changed dramatically. Daddy told me that he was very sick, but I didn't know at the time how seriously. He assured me that he was following the doctor's orders and that everything would be all right. But he wasn't strong enough to go to his garage every day as he used to. Some days he was able to work, but on others he simply stayed in bed. I began to worry and to pray for his recovery.

One day when Daddy had trouble breathing, Mother told me to get the doctor. I ran all the way to his house, though she had meant for me to get him on the telephone! By the time I arrived, I was so out of breath that I couldn't even tell him why I had come. But the doctor knew. He put me in his car and we drove back home to see about my father.

My father's condition worsened. He didn't have the strength to get out of bed. Often he would call me and my brothers and sister into his room to talk about what we had been doing during the day or to report on our progress in school. I wanted to let him know how much I loved him, so I tried to do everything for him. I combed his hair and read detective stories to him. I would bring my books into his room to study, but I couldn't concentrate. And I remember being afraid all the time —afraid of what was going to happen.

Religion played an important role in our lives. We used to gather around Daddy's bed, and someone would read the Bible out loud. Our preacher came often to visit, and one day he told Mother that goat's milk would make my father better. So we bought a goat. We children fed it and my mother milked it every day, but it didn't help. When a loved one is desperately ill, one is willing to try anything.

My mother's parents, Mama and Papa Murray, came often. Toward the end, they were at our house daily and were a great help with the small children and a support for my mother. Being an only child and marrying a man who was nine years older, Mother had led a sheltered life. Before my father's illness, she had had little experience of dealing with the world— Daddy had taken care of everything. The severe adversity she was about to encounter was completely foreign to her.

Any time there's a crisis, such as my father's fight with leukemia, in a town as small as Plains (with only six hundred residents), everyone gets involved. Our friends and neighbors were wonderful. Jimmy's mother, Miss Lillian, was a nurse. She came daily to give Daddy shots or whatever other help he needed. One day, after weeks of trying, she even talked Mother into going to a movie with her.

Today, Mother recalls Miss Lillian asking her on the way

home, "You didn't really enjoy the movie at all, did you?" And Mother said she had to answer no.

Other townsfolk helped us too. Someone was always bringing in food and the men from downtown would take turns sitting with Daddy. When he became very ill, they would help Mother turn him in bed. By then, Mother had also hired a woman to help with the cooking and the heavy work. Jesse Mae Wallace laundered my father's bed linens in a big black washpot over a fire in the backyard. People were in our house at all hours of the night and day.

At thirteen, I had mixed feelings about this. I'm sure it helped us to have the neighbors around. But often I just wished they would go away. Every day when I came home from school, someone was there. I wanted to be alone with my family—to grieve with them. I didn't feel like being strong or putting on a "company face" all the time. I wanted to be able to cry. The only way I could do that was to run to my secret crying place—the outdoor privy.

When I spoke to my mother recently about this difficult period in our lives, she agreed that she and even my father had been ambivalent about having so many visitors. Although they deeply appreciated their neighbors' help, they felt that they had to be gracious and hospitable toward them when they really were not feeling up to it, and that sapped them of precious energy and time to be alone with each other.

After a valiant but futile struggle with leukemia, my father, Wilburn Edgar Smith, died in October of 1940 at the age of forty-four. He left my thirty-four-year-old mother with few financial resources and four small children ranging in age from four to thirteen. But that wasn't the end of our sorrows or our experience with caregiving.

TAKING CARE OF PAPA

Eleven months after my father's death, Mama Murray died suddenly. On that September morning, Papa had risen early to milk the cows, as was his habit. Mama was busy getting dressed. When Papa returned from the barn, he found her leaning over in a chair. It seemed as though she had been stricken while tying her shoes.

Another tragedy for our family. We were still grieving over the loss of my father and had depended on Mama and Papa so much. Mama had been at our house often to help Mother with us children, to comfort her—and us. Now she was gone, and we felt lost without her. And my poor grandfather was distraught. At the age of seventy, he didn't know what to do without her, and he didn't want to live alone. Within a few months of Mama's death, he left the farm—the only home he had ever known—and moved in with us. My mother cared for him for the next twenty-five years, until he died at the age of ninety-five.

My memories of him are of his always being there, sitting on the porch, speaking to everyone who passed by, or sitting at the breakfast room table reading the Bible. For years he also walked to town every day—one long block—to see "what's going on."

Recently, I asked Mother if Papa was a help to her during that time. "It was nice to have his company," she replied, "but if I asked his advice, he would always say, 'You can decide.' " Papa leaned on her for strength, as we all did, and left the full burden of responsibility for the family, including him, on her.

And he sometimes behaved in ways that were frustrating.

One day Papa came into the kitchen and proudly announced to Mother, "Allie, I sold your cow. I just couldn't stand to see you working so hard." But we needed the income the cow brought to our family. My mother and the boys took turns milking it, and I helped churn. We then sold some of the milk and butter to augment our meager income. Mother cried at Papa's short-sightedness, but she didn't let him see her. She told us not to tell him how much he had upset her. She didn't want to hurt his feelings.

My mother had to go to work to support us and care for her father. She had various jobs: sewing for others, working in the school lunchroom, then in a grocery store. And while I was still in high school, she got a part-time job at the post office. Eventually she worked there full-time.

Although she put in a forty-hour week, the postmaster arranged for her to work what we would now call "flex-time." She arrived at work every morning at seven and could go home for several hours in the middle of the day to make sure Papa was all right. One of our neighbors also dropped in from time to time during the day to check on him. And after he became bedridden, Mother found someone to stay with him while she worked.

This flexible arrangement had its advantages. Mother could work, but still care for Papa, prepare his main meal of the day, and just be company for him. It relieved her anxiety about being away and also gave Papa something to look forward to during the day.

But the arrangement also had its disadvantages. The postmaster came to depend on Mother to be at the post office before everyone else in the mornings and after normal working hours in the afternoons. He didn't give her a day off—ever.

She took no vacations except legal holidays. Even on Saturdays, when the regular windows were closed, she was required to wait on customers through a side door.

Because of the demands of her work and her responsibilities caring for Papa and the younger children, my mother was completely tied down for years. Once, after Papa was really sick, but before he was bedridden, she went to visit my sister, who had recently married and moved away from home, and I cared for him for a few days. I learned to appreciate how much she had to do. And that occasion was the only time I can remember Mother ever having a break.

In fact, the first time I recall her having any fun at all was at the age of seventy, when Jimmy was campaigning for the White House. Papa had died in 1966, during Jimmy's first gubernatorial campaign, and government regulations forced Mother into retirement in 1975. Having become so used to working night and day, she felt miserable and useless at first. But soon she became involved in our 1976 presidential campaign and made many new friends. She even began working a few hours each day delivering flowers for the local florist shop because she needed something to do. This kept her in touch with those in our community who were sick and shut-in.

After Jimmy was elected president, Mother traveled a lot with her friends, coming to the White House on occasion to see us, enjoying herself. For the first time in her life, she was free.

Still, it saddens me to think that my mother was more than seventy years old before she had any kind of life of her own. For as my grandfather aged, his needs grew. During the last few years of his life, he couldn't get around by himself. He would sit in a chair, but only if someone helped him up and down.

And it was always an ordeal to manage his bathroom needs. Papa was terribly embarrassed when Mother helped him to the toilet. She repeatedly asked him to wake her at night if he needed help, but he resisted her requests. He always worried that he was bothering her, and he was humiliated that she should be involved in such private matters. But after he fell once in the middle of the night, he finally decided he had to awaken her.

When I recently asked my mother if she had ever felt burned out—as if she just couldn't take care of Papa anymore—she replied with some surprise, "Why, no. Papa was easy to get along with." But then after a few minutes she recalled the difficult times during the last few years of his life. As he grew weaker, Papa could no longer leave his bed. Although in previous years she had urged him to call for help when he needed it, and he had refrained for fear of imposing on her, now he kept her up half the night with his cries. "That was really hard on me," she said. "I still had to be at the post office at seven o'clock every morning to work."

MY OWN EXPERIENCES WITH CAREGIVING

I never realized that I too was a caregiver until I became involved with the Rosalynn Carter Institute's caregiving program. Using my mother's experiences with Daddy and Papa as models, I had always thought of caregivers as those who are responsible for the day-in, day-out nursing care of a sick or elderly family member living at home. But that's not necessarily true. People who are responsible for a loved one, even though they're not living together, are also caregivers. They still help out and check in. Caregiving becomes part of their lives, even if they devote only a small amount of time to their loved one.

That's my situation now. I'm always thinking about whether my mother is okay. As I write this book, she is in her late eighties and lives alone. She still drives her car, although we worry about it. My mother is fairly independent, but she requires a watchful eye, nonetheless.

Recently she has had some serious medical problems including a clogged carotid artery that required surgery, fainting spells, and, most frightening of all, congestive heart failure. Luckily I happened to be home when she had the heart problem and was able to rush her to the hospital. She is better now and stays with us sometimes when we are home, but when it comes to her health, I can never rest easy.

And my mother is frightened too. Mostly she is afraid that something will happen to her at night when she's alone, and nobody will know about it. It's an understandable fear. Although my brother and his wife, who live in Plains, check in with her all the time and have set up a room for her in their home, she still wants me around. I'm her oldest child, the daughter living near her. Unfortunately my activities at the Carter Center in Atlanta and the Rosalynn Carter Institute in Americus require that I travel a lot. Still, it's hard for me to be gone, especially since I know that Mother wants me to be at home.

MY CAREER IN MENTAL HEALTH

Although it seems as if I have been closely associated with caregiving nearly all of my life, I first embraced the issues formally when Jimmy ran for governor in 1970. All along the campaign trail, I encountered people—among them many care-givers—who willingly and openly shared their stories and their pain with me. They were tending a terminally ill parent or spouse with little financial support; they had a mentally ill child at home and didn't know how to cope. Many asked me what my husband would do to help them if he became governor.

I was particularly moved by the plight of a woman who emerged from a cotton mill at four-thirty one morning. I was standing at the gate, handing out campaign brochures as the shift changed, when I spoke to her. Her hair and sweater were covered with lint. She had been working all night. She ex-plained to me that she had a mentally ill daughter at home and that her husband's salary didn't cover the extra expenses that their child's condition generated. She had to work to make ends meet.

"Are you going home to sleep now?" I asked.

She replied, "I'll nap some during the day, but I have to take care of Margaret."

Suddenly I felt great empathy for this woman—working at night, taking care of a disabled child during the day while she tried to get some rest. Indeed, she reminded me of my mother, who had never had any time of her own. If Jimmy did win the election, was there anything I could do to help her?

I knew I would need some activities to occupy me if Jimmy were to become governor. I had worked for many years in our farm supply business, keeping the books and helping run our financial affairs. I was used to working. Also, Jimmy had been in the State Senate for four years, and I was aware of the great need for improvement in the mental health system in Georgia. That very morning at the cotton mill I decided that if Jimmy was elected, this would be a worthwhile project for me: trying to make life easier for those suffering from mental illnesses—and for their families.

During the race for the governorship, we didn't have formal schedules, as we had later in the presidential election campaign. By chance, one day I discovered that Jimmy would be in the same town that I was campaigning in, for an evening event. He was to make a speech at a big rally, so I decided to stay and see him. I stood in the back of the crowd during his presentation. When he finished speaking, I stepped into the receiving line with everyone else. Shaking one hand and then another, he reached out for mine before he saw who I was.

"What are you doing here?" he exclaimed.

"I came to see what you are going to do about mental health when you are governor."

He replied, "We're going to have the best mental health system in the country, and I'm going to put you in charge of it."

And he kept his word, mostly. Shortly after his inauguration, Jimmy formed the Governor's Commission to Improve Services to the Mentally and Emotionally Handicapped. But I did not chair it because I lacked sufficient knowledge of the issues to help in a substantive way. I did, however, become a member of the commission along with mental health professionals, laypeople, parents, and other concerned citizens. Thus began my formal education about the problems of those suffering from mental illnesses.

I attended all the commission meetings, volunteered one day a week at Georgia Regional Hospital, and toured the other state mental institutions, reporting my findings to the commission. I listened and I learned.

Over the next four years, we made much progress in the mental health program in our state, shifting the emphasis of care from large impersonal institutions to smaller community-based group homes and mental health centers. When properly implemented, this process of deinstitutionalization is a more humane system of caring for those who are afflicted with mental illnesses, allowing them to live at home with their families and yet have somewhere to go during the day for care.

My efforts on behalf of mentally ill people continued during and after the presidential campaign of 1976. It had been fifteen years since the federal government had seriously studied the U.S. mental health system. Programs were fragmented and fraught with bureaucratic problems. Despite its humane goals, deinstitutionalization had a major failing: people were being turned out of institutions throughout the country without adequate community programs in place.

I felt it was time to assess the system and draw up a new national policy of mental health care. The only campaign promise I ever made for him was that if elected president, Jimmy would set up a commission to study mental health issues. He followed through again.

Less than a month after we moved into the White House, I held my first press conference to announce the President's Commission on Mental Health. First ladies have enormous influence just because of their proximity to power. I would have the help of those in our country best qualified to develop a new program, and I would have access to officials at the highest levels of government. I also hoped that if I could focus attention on the issue, I might be able to overcome some of the stigma associated with mental illness that keeps many who suffer from seeking help. Again, this time because of nepotism laws, I couldn't chair the commission, so I became an active honorary chairperson. My main project as first lady was to develop a strategy to provide better care for people with mental illness.

The commission held hearings and conducted studies in the areas of access to care, quality of care, prevention, research, and the needs of people with chronic mental illness. With the eventual passage of the Mental Health Systems Act of 1980, we tried to correct many problems, including inadequately funded community-based programs, unwieldy government regulations, lack of insurance coverage, scanty research in child and adolescent psychopathology, and nonexistent preventative programs. Unfortunately, many of the advances we made were reversed by the Reagan administration shortly after Jimmy left office.

Although mental health has been my main area of focus over the years, I have spent much time on other important issues— in particular, problems of the elderly and women's issues. The concerns of these two groups have given me further insight into the needs and problems of caregivers.

As a result of Jimmy's political activities, I had a great deal of contact with older Americans. Supporters in a community take campaigners to places where people are congregated, so I visited convalescent homes, Golden Age clubs, and Senior Citizen Centers in communities all over my state and, later, the country. Most often, the older people were Democrats, particularly those who resided in public facilities and were on Medicare and Medicaid.

These citizens talked to me about their problems: of dependency, illness, loneliness, fear, feelings of uselessness and helplessness. And I found during my involvement with the President's Commission on Mental Health that there were few professionals specially trained to meet the emotional and even the medical needs of older people. During our time in the White House, I lobbied for passage of the Age Discrimination Act, the Older Americans Act, and Social Security Disability Amendments, among other pieces of legislation.

My work on women's issues included supporting flex-time schedules for women in the federal government and expanded day-care centers. And I worked very hard to get the Equal Rights Amendment passed. Today, I consider that failure as one of my greatest disappointments.

MENTAL HEALTH AND CAREGIVING

Although it may not be immediately apparent, an interest in mental health includes an involvement in issues relating to caregiving. For the term *mental health* does not refer only to severe mental illnesses such as schizophrenia and manic depression. It also pertains to quality-of-life issues: marital disruption, delinquent children, drug or alcohol abuse, the inability to deal with death or a serious accident or illness, depression, and low self-esteem. Research has shown that family caregivers can suffer from many of these problems because of their difficult situation.

The emotional costs of caregiving can be high. According to a national survey published in 1987, by the Select Committee on Aging, many caregivers experience a limited social life, infringement of privacy, and sleep deprivation as a result of providing care. Indeed, many found the task physically and emotionally taxing, especially when they had to lift their loved one or endure his or her agitation, confusion, or dementia-related behavior.

As a result, when compared with the general population, caregivers were three times more likely to be depressed, two to three times more likely to take psychotropic drugs (such as tranquilizers), and 12 percent more likely to use alcohol as a way to cope with stress.

Other studies have shown that caregivers typically experience chronic emotional and physical fatigue; family and marital conflicts; social isolation, including loss of friends, recreational opportunities, privacy, and hobbies; and feelings of anger, guilt, grief, resentment, hopelessness, and anxiety. Dwindling finances can lead to despair. Research also indicates that family caregivers are at high risk for work absenteeism and poor health themselves because of the intense stress they must endure.

Moreover, the stigma of a loved one's ailment can rub off on the caregiver, especially if the person is suffering from mental illness, AIDS, or even cancer. But even when there is no stigma, caregivers often feel that no one is interested in or cares about *them* and *their* needs and concerns. All of the attention focuses on the ill family member. The caregivers feel that they don't get much cooperation or respect from doctors, either. And friends may drop in, but do so out of a sense of duty rather than love.

Clearly, caregivers have problems of their own that deserve attention and study. My many years of work in the mental health field have convinced me of the importance of focusing on the caregiving process. It may be possible to help a loved one avoid additional pain and suffering and prevent caregivers from becoming casualties themselves.

And so, in 1988, when Dr. William Capitan, president of Georgia Southwestern College, approached me with a proposal to establish the Rosalynn Carter Institute for Human Development, it seemed natural for us to use the Institute to look into caregiving—this often ignored but highly significant aspect of mental health.

In the following chapter, I'll tell you more about the Institute's activities and the research we are currently conducting in the field of caregiving.

3.

$\mathscr{C}$AREGIVING
IN THE NINETIES

Despite the many difficulties caregiving presented my mother when she was caring for her father, she was still fortunate in some ways. Her widowed neighbor and distant relative, May Wise, would look in on my grandfather from time to time during the day while Mother worked. Aunt May, as we called her, even spent nights with her to help with Papa's bathroom and other needs. Her involvement relieved some of Mother's anxiety. And Mother's arrangement with the postmaster, which allowed her to spend a few hours at home with Papa in the middle of the day, also helped.

But times have changed. Who among us has neighbors like Aunt May who can pitch in? As I have learned more about the issue, I have come to realize how serious the crisis in caregiving is today. More people need care, and fewer are available to give it or to assist in its delivery. And so the burden on the primary caregiver is greater than ever.

THE CAREGIVING CRISIS

Many factors have contributed to today's caregiving crisis. Families aren't as closely knit or as large as they once were. Half of all marriages taking place in the 1990s will end in divorce. In addition, many people marry later and have fewer children. As a result, the pool of potential caregivers is diminishing.

Furthermore, the traditional nuclear family is being replaced by more complex structures such as step-, blended, and single-parent families in which ties of allegiance and caregiving roles may be unclear. An adult stepdaughter, for example, may be torn between caring for her widowed stepmother and her biological mother. Even within intact families, grown children move away from home and may be unavailable to help or to take charge when the need arises. Or if they do attempt long-distance caregiving, they do so at great personal cost.

Women have always been the traditional caregivers in our society, yet today more and more of them work. In the 1940s, only one out of seven married women worked outside the home; today about half of all married women do. Because of work-related responsibilities and stress, women have less time and energy to devote to family caregiving. Moreover, large numbers of disadvantaged children are being raised in single-parent homes in which mothers must work to support the family. And when a disabled child lives in a home, the mother's burden is even greater. (There is more on women's dilemmas in Chapter 8.)

Other social factors also contribute to the crisis. The deinstitutionalization of those with mental illness means that more of these individuals are cared for within the community. Their families must provide most of their long-term care. And the hundreds of thousands of men and women suffering from AIDS require increasing assistance as that devastating disease takes its toll.

Today, in cities and even in small communities across the nation, neighbors are not available to look in on a loved one who is ailing. People are so busy, caught up in making a living and the other things they must do, that they don't have the time they once had to care for those who require help. These days, it is rare for a community to pull together when one of its members becomes ill, as the folks in Plains did when my father was sick.

Ironically, this crisis in caregiving has been compounded by advances in medical science. Improved nutrition, disease control, lifestyle choices (such as giving up smoking), and life-prolonging technology mean that our life expectancy is greater than ever. Whereas at the turn of the century, forty-five was thought a normal lifespan, today death before the age of sixty-five is considered premature. Now Americans can easily anticipate living to the age of seventy-five or more. Every week, according to the latest research, our life expectancy goes up two days. Perhaps our great-grandchildren will even attain the biblical age of 120!

That's good news for all of us, yet such advances also mean that the number of frail elderly individuals living with chronic conditions is on the rise. More children and adults survive serious trauma or illness than ever before, but oftentimes they require care for the rest of their lives. Situations now arise in which people in their seventies, who themselves may need attention, are caring for parents in their nineties.

The changes that have taken place in our society have put a great strain on caregivers. And yet family members continue to care for the vast majority of dependent people at home.

BUREAUCRACY ADDS TO THE CRISIS

Family caregivers who are trying to provide help are frequently overwhelmed by a task for which they feel unprepared. After all, this is not a role they rehearse before the need arises. One of their more stressful problems consists of being caught up in our nation's chaotic and entangling health-care bureaucracy: caregivers don't know where to go or how to get help for themselves and their loved one.

Dr. Jack Nottingham, a psychology professor at Georgia Southwestern College and the director of the Rosalynn Carter Institute, knows the situation firsthand. When his ailing father could no longer care for his mother, who was suffering from Alzheimer's, he suddenly found himself confronting what he called the "organizational disconnectiveness, compartmentalization, dehumanization, and inefficiency" of the health-care system.

"Even though we had professional expertise, personal resourcefulness, and knowledge of community resources," Dr. Nottingham explained, "we were not able to cope very well. We felt ill prepared and inadequate for our hands-on caregiving roles. These experiences made us wonder about the fate of other family caregivers who did not have the same professional advantage we believed we had."

Dr. Nottingham's concerns are valid. If professionals in the field of caregiving have difficulty finding their bearings when thrust into the role, imagine how poorly those who have little preparation must fare.

One of my young friends was married for about two years when her husband developed a mental illness. At first Elizabeth didn't want anybody to know about her situation. But when it became unbearable, she began making the rounds of public health service organizations. She was sent from one agency to another and was absolutely and totally lost when she finally appealed to me for help. I was able to assist her in finding help, mostly by getting her in touch with the National Alliance for the Mentally Ill, a wonderful support group. But I still worry. How many other Elizabeths are out there who just don't know where to turn?

Indeed, in 1992, at the Fourth Annual Conference of the Rosalynn Carter Institute, Virginia Schiaffino, a clinical social worker and the executive director of the National Federation of Interfaith Volunteer Caregivers, Inc., came to talk with us about congregation-based volunteer caregivers. In the midst of her presentation, she paused and shared her personal story of frustration.

About five years earlier, her father had become homebound with heart disease. Her mother didn't drive. As the geographically closest sibling, Ms. Schiaffino took responsibility for helping her parents, even though she lived an hour from their home and worked a full-time job that required travel around the country. She was dismayed at what she found.

"Although there were five of us children," she told us, "two social workers, a physician, a college professor, and a sister who worked for the leading law firm in New York City, we were all baffled by the system. And when I went to my parents' congregation and asked, 'Don't you have something that can help our parents?' I received a pat on the back and was told, 'Call Sister So-and-So. . . . Maybe she can find something to help you out.' That did not respond to my needs, and it certainly didn't respond to anyone else's needs in the family."

Today's caregivers must cope with dwindling family resources and confusing regulations; with religious institutions that are unresponsive to real-life problems; with a health-care system that ignores their input, gives them the runaround, and even penalizes them if they wish to care for a loved one at home.

Helping another human being can be an extremely rewarding experience, but it can also be a traumatic one. When caregivers suffer, the quality of care they're able to provide diminishes. And if they continue to be excessively burdened, they too may become casualties—physically, socially, and psychologically—and may even require care themselves.

It is my hope that the Rosalynn Carter Institute for Human Development (RCI) will bring all of these important issues into the foreground for study in an effort to provide some relief for those who undertake care of another.

THE ROSALYNN CARTER INSTITUTE

Originally the goals of the Rosalynn Carter Institute were quite general: the Institute was created to improve research and teaching in human development and mental health. But soon after its establishment we began to focus exclusively on the caregiving aspects of human development.

Now the mission of the Rosalynn Carter Institute is to understand the caregiving process and discover new ways to assist formal and informal caregivers. We are concentrating on the difficulties and rewards experienced by caregivers who help those with

- emotional and mental problems
- dilemmas associated with aging
- developmental disabilities
- physical illnesses

We have also decided to emphasize preventive mental health care. Recognizing that caregiving is often an exceedingly stressful burden, we feel it is preferable to help caregivers nip problems in the bud rather than wait until they become overwhelming. To that end, the Institute is currently developing caregiver training programs for family members and professionals, support groups for caregivers, and a resource center to provide information and referrals. (There is more on these subjects in Chapter 7.)

The Institute also sponsors conferences; formulates social policy; distributes information; coordinates efforts by researchers, community leaders, public officials, health professionals, and interest groups; and provides further professional training in caregiving issues.

As we were preparing for our first conference in 1988, we realized the importance of caregiving, and how much good might come from bringing together people who are in the same situation so that they can learn from one another, recount experiences, exchange ideas, and gain encouragement. We decided it might be helpful to bring together family and professional caregivers to interact with one another, and we made plans accordingly.

Our inaugural conference was even more successful than we had hoped it would be. As formal and informal caregivers began to connect on a personal level, they shared their stories. Many expressed feelings of isolation and loneliness. We had searched out many family caregivers who were shut in because of their responsibilities and made arrangements for them to be with us. It was the first time some family caregivers had ever revealed their burdens to others. There is so much burnout among caregivers. It can be great therapy just to air feelings and experiences.

One man's life was turned around just by participating in an RCI conference. Truman Davis was caring for his wife, who had Alzheimer's disease. When asked if he would be willing to tell his story to the entire conference, he said he didn't think he was different from everyone else, that what he was doing as a caregiver was not all that special and he hadn't known that anyone cared.

Our liaison, Diane Red of the Greater Columbus Alzheimer's Association, assured him that he was very special and that someone did care. She talked him into participating.

At the conference, Mr. Davis got up before me and the whole audience and told his story. When he finished, I said, "Mr. Davis, you have brought tears to my eyes and those of everyone in the room with your story, and I thank you."

Mr. Davis was proud that his story could make a difference and that I had acknowledged it. Now, at eighty-one, walking with a cane, he is dedicated to helping other caregivers by volunteering *every day* at the Alzheimer's Association office in Columbus. His wife's disease progressed to the point where she had to be placed in a nursing home, but his life has new meaning because at the conference he learned that he was special and that others cared.

Experiences such as these, which demonstrated the great need for help for caregivers in our area, inspired us. One of our first actions, in 1990, was to form the West Central Georgia Caregivers Network—CARE-NET for short—as a demonstration project to show how informal and formal caregivers can cooperate and share responsibility for dependent or partly dependent individuals. CARE-NET serves more than 330,000 people in a sixteen-county area. Informal and formal caregiver representatives from the whole region sit on a coordinating council. The council decides on programs for the RCI, makes plans for carrying them out, and monitors their progress.

What is so important and remarkable about CARE-NET is its depth and diversity. We have professional caregivers; family caregivers; representatives of local, state, and federal government agencies; representatives of the religious community; advocates; and other concerned citizens sitting down together, talking about the problems involved and trying to find ways to resolve them.

At the RCI, we also decided to explore what resources there were for information and help on a national level. I began calling the leaders of mental and physical health–related organizations around the country: the American Association of Retired Persons (AARP), the National Mental Health Association, the National Alliance for the Mentally Ill (NAMI), the American Nurses Association, the American Medical Association, the American Psychiatric Association, the American Psychological Association, and the National Association of Social Workers, among others. We wanted to know if there were models already established from which the Rosalynn Carter Institute could benefit.

I called about twenty-five or thirty of these groups and learned that no organization was focusing on the lives of caregivers across the spectrum of illnesses and needs. The National Alliance for the Mentally Ill gives advice and support to the families of people with mental illness. Some of the other organizations have programs for their members, but none looks at caregiving generically. All of the leaders of these organizations thought that this was an important and timely issue, one that needed to be pursued. Many wanted to help with it.

As a result of these contacts, we formed the National Quality Caregiving Coalition (NQCC). Representatives from these organizations meet with the board of the Rosalynn Carter Institute every year. The RCI gets ideas from NQCC members and keeps them informed about the progress of our programs. Together we have created an alliance of concerned professionals and laypersons and are now working to develop a plan that will include a central caregivers' information resource center, a national newsletter, and regular conferences on caregiving.

As I have traveled the country and spoken about my involvement in caregiving, people now call or write to me asking about the RCI program. And I am happy to tell them some of the things we are doing. But perhaps our most exciting work has been in researching caregivers' needs and experiences.

THE CARE-NET STUDY:
A UNIQUE UNDERTAKING

The members of the CARE-NET Leadership Council realized that in order to truly help caregivers, they first needed to have a profound understanding and appreciation of their characteristics, obligations, and concerns. And so the Council appointed a "needs assessment" committee, which undertook an ambitious study of formal and informal caregivers in West Central Georgia over a two-year period.

There have been many well-intentioned efforts to address community needs in the past. Experts from universities, government agencies, and similar institutions have tried to find answers to the problems that caregivers face. Often, however, research has focused on a particular population—formal versus informal caregivers or those caring for people with Alzheimer's versus those helping people with cancer—rather than on caregiving across the board. We were interested in identifying the common bonds that unite *all* caregivers. What is it like to be a caregiver in the 1990s? What are the challenges and rewards?

In addition, "experts" often remain aloof in their ivory towers —very much separated from the people they are trying to assess and serve. So we vowed not to detach ourselves from the real world. We did not want to diagnose problems and decide how to remedy them without actually *asking* the most affected individuals and groups what their lives are like, and what they believed could be done to help them. Without posing these basic questions, we ran the risk of establishing programs that would fail to address the needs of the very people we were trying to help.

In light of these observations, the CARE-NET committee decided on our approach to the assessment. First, without making any assumptions, we engaged in a concerted effort to ask caregivers directly about their lives and needs. We appealed to actual caregivers from the CARE-NET Council—family members as well as professionals—to help us develop and fine-tune interview and survey questions.

Second, a number of family caregivers joined the planning committee as it prepared to do the research. They contributed some good ideas that had never occurred to the professional staff. For example, one participant suggested that all family caregivers converge at a single location to be interviewed. After their separate interviews, they would then be able to connect with one another at a group lunch, to discuss their experiences —a plan we adopted. Indeed, the professional members of the committee agreed that despite their preconceived notions, they had as much to learn from the lay members of the committee as they had to teach.

Finally, the committee realized that the way in which the research was conducted was at least as important as the results themselves. So we enlisted family caregivers, assisted by college students, to interview the formal caregivers: physicians, nurses, psychologists, social workers, clergy, nurses' aides, mental retardation specialists, and drug rehabilitation counselors, among others. Conversely we recruited community-based professionals to go with college students to interview informal caregivers: family members, friends, and concerned citizens.

Much healing and empathy occurred in these exchanges of ideas, information, and experiences. As Dr. Nottingham and his research team explain in their written report on the study, many informal caregivers seemed to take enormous pride in having been selected to participate in the project. Most spent a great deal of time interacting with other caregivers. In some instances, the interviewers and interviewees even hugged one another or cried together as the tales unfolded.

Our research team noted, "Many family caregivers seemed to gain a sense of emotional support from 'telling their stories' and having had the opportunity to visit and share their experience with other caregivers." All in all, the research itself became a part of the healing process—and that meant a lot to us.

While I can't go into all of the details here, I would like to share with you some of what the research team found, especially as it relates to family or informal caregivers.

WHO PARTICIPATED

Drawing from four representative counties in the sixteen-county area of West Central Georgia, the research team located 543 informal caregivers. Of these, they randomly selected 175 to take part in our study.

Participants were given an extensive questionnaire that inquired about burnout, isolation, recognition from the media or other outside sources, assistance from agencies and religious institutions, family communication, depression, education and training, stress management, and support systems, among other issues. Participants also rated the adequacy and importance of certain resources such as financial assistance, personal counseling, and linkage with other caregivers now and in the future.

Then, forty-nine of these family caregivers were randomly selected for further study. Local formal caregivers and college students interviewed this group at greater length to determine how they were coping with their caregiving responsibilities.

What We Wanted to Know

For the sake of consistency, the interviewers all asked the same questions, including:

- How do you spend a typical week, including how much time you devote to caregiving?
- How long have you been providing care?
- How did you become involved in caregiving? Was your involvement voluntary?
- What kind of assistance do you furnish?
- How much help do you receive from others, including family members, religious institutions, and professional agencies?
- In what ways do you feel your caregiving makes a difference?
- Did you have prior caregiving experiences?
- How well do you get along with the person you are caring for, and has the relationship improved or deteriorated over time?
- What were your best and worst caregiving experiences with your family member?
- Have your feelings toward caregiving (and the person you are caring for) changed as a result of your activities?
- What were your good and bad experiences with professionals and agencies and what suggestions might you make to improve the interaction between informal and formal caregivers?
- What do you think professionals need in order to do their job better?
- What advice would you give other informal caregivers?

- Has caregiving changed your life?
- In what areas could you use more education or training?
- What services or resources would make your life easier?
- Who would take over caregiving if you were no longer able to provide it?
- What do you think are the proper roles of family, professionals, and patient?
- What do you find enjoyable or relaxing in your life?

You might want to ask yourself these same questions to help you determine how you're doing.

WHAT WE FOUND

The CARE-NET study revealed a rich panoply of voices. People of all socioeconomic groups and all walks of life participated. They cared for family members, friends, and even strangers. Some felt their caregiving was a duty and a burden, others that it was a privilege and a blessing, and for many it was a little bit of both. In fact, after analyzing all the information, the research team compared caregiving to running a marathon race: it is at the same time arduous and yet satisfying.

Our study yielded some statistics that you might find interesting, especially if they validate your own experiences:

- Eighty percent of the informal caregivers were women. This is consistent with women's traditional roles and the results of other studies in the field.
- Sixty-one percent of the caregivers were married.
- More than a third had been engaged in caregiving activities

for more than ten years. (This is of particular concern, since caregiving is such a stressful activity.)

- Forty-one percent spent more than forty hours a week providing care, yet 90 percent worked outside the home for pay. However, about one-third missed a month or more of work over their entire caregiving experience.
- Nearly 75 percent of the caregivers reported that they provided *all* or most of the care for their loved one.
- More than 50 percent of the caregivers turned first to other family members for assistance, yet sadly, nearly 66 percent reported receiving no help or very little help from them. Only 16 percent said they sought help most often from public or private agencies.
- Fifty percent of the caregivers reported that they were probably experiencing burnout.

Looking at these statistics and the fact that most caregivers already hold down full-time jobs in order to support themselves and their families financially, you can understand why many informal caregivers in our study referred to their lives as "hectic." Most saw themselves as busy individuals who juggled multiple responsibilities. One woman even commented that her husband and children regarded her as "superwoman" because of all the responsibilities she managed.

Furthermore, when spare time was available, many of the informal caregivers we interviewed reported that they were too tired to luxuriate in rest or relaxation. Peter, for example, was quite depressed about his wife's deteriorating condition due to a brain tumor. He had no hobbies or outlets. "I cannot escape the situation," Peter said. "Sometimes I read and farm, but most of the time I isolate myself from everyone."

Only a minority reported that they enjoyed a wide variety of outside interests. Not surprisingly, these individuals seemed to have a more positive response to their role. Indeed, our study revealed that the degree of satisfaction experienced by caregivers did not relate to the number of hours they put in or the number of people they cared for, but rather to *the caregivers' ability to care for themselves*. (More on that in Chapter 8.)

Caregiving encompasses a multitude of activities. Large percentages of the informal caregivers in our study engaged in taxing, potentially unpleasant tasks such as housekeeping or personal hygiene (bathing, dressing, attending to bodily functions). Our research indicated that informal caregivers who provide this kind of arduous help—especially without a good support system—tend to experience burnout more often than those who don't. Paula, caring for her father, for example, was most graphic in her description of her burdens:

> My father required total care. Feeding, dressing, changing dressings on bedsores, enemas. He was an invalid and couldn't do anything. I did this for one month . . . then hired someone to come in a couple of hours each day to help. I had to bathe him, check his blood pressure, put him to bed, monitor his medications, catheter him, and do rectal checks every day. The hired help reduced the load considerably, but I always felt responsible for the right decisions.

Other activities that caregivers in the CARE-NET study engaged in included:

- companionship ("sitting with") and emotional or moral support—activities that could be rewarding yet involve no financial cost

- transportation
- shopping
- monitoring health and welfare and administering medication
- preparing meals
- lifting and assisting with movement
- scheduling medical appointments
- tending to pets
- paying bills
- acting as an advocate

Despite their many responsibilities, however, some caregivers were quite reluctant to call upon others to help them or they were rather critical of how others performed caregiving duties. Maria, for example, complained that her father-in-law was "too lenient" in providing care to her mentally ill, obese stepson, allowing him to eat whenever and whatever he wanted.

Conversely, other caregivers complained that family members did not help enough. Gil charged that his cousins might volunteer to help with his retarded daughter, but "they are not really sincere or interested." And Frances told the difficult tale of how a long-planned and much-needed vacation was nearly canceled because the sister who was supposed to take over the care of their invalid mother during Frances's absence had problems keeping her commitment. When the arrangements finally worked out, Frances told her family, "Don't contact me under any circumstances while I'm gone. Not even if Mother dies." Clearly this woman needed a break!

Yet despite these difficulties, informal caregivers were still more likely to turn to family members, neighbors, or fellow church members to secure aid than they were to go to agencies or other organizations for support. As Charles, the brother of a mentally ill young man, put it, "I don't turn to outside people because they want to know your business but not share your problems."

Of course, many caregivers also recognized that the amount of assistance they receive is largely dependent on their willingness to ask for it. When our interviewers inquired about advice the study participants could offer other caregivers, many responded that people should ask for help if they need it. Suzanne said, "People shouldn't be martyrs. They should have enough help." Bob said, "Take time for yourself. Ask for help in the home." And Anna added, "Don't think you are the only one who can provide care; share the responsibility of care; demand help of family members."

Carol was fortunate to develop an extensive informal support system that helped her get through the rough spots.

> I have a couple of friends, both of my sisters, and my daughter who support me. I feel well supported. I have four cats who are a big help. I love my work. It's very restorative. I also have my minister. . . . I have lots of interaction with others.

Even in a time of shrinking resources, Carol seemed to have equipped herself well to deal with her caregiving responsibilities.

And many caregivers responded that they turned to their religious faith for strength.

THE GOOD, THE BAD,
AND THE UGLY

The participants in our study were quite candid when discussing the burden of responsibilities. Their answers did not describe caregiving as a completely ennobling experience, nor did they paint themselves as unsung heroes. Many saw themselves doing a job that had to be done, but growing from the experience in the process. Some caregivers, though, were quite vocal about the harsh realities of caregiving and their frustrations with it.

Understandably, one of the most difficult experiences for caregivers occurs when their loved one sustains a setback or when his or her physical or mental condition slowly deteriorates. Peter, whose wife was suffering from a brain tumor, explained that the worst part of caregiving for him was "to watch Janice go from a productive, competent person to an incompetent, nonproductive individual" who no longer recognized or responded to him. Other caregivers complained about the unpleasant task of cleaning up after an incontinent parent, helplessly watching a loved one in pain, or having to face the fact that their kin was declining physically or dying.

Others felt great frustration and resentment at the lack of recognition or gratitude from the person they were caring for. Faye, for example, felt so overwhelmed with her father's demands and constant criticism ("In his eyes, I couldn't do anything right") that one day she packed her bags and checked into a motel in town.

"Can you imagine?" she said remorsefully. "I left a helpless old man alone in a wheelchair." Gripped by guilt, she returned after a few hours, telling her father that she had become tied up in town. But she was still unhappy about her situation. "I went back only because I had to," she admitted.

Other caregivers complained about unreliable help and incompetent, dehumanizing medical care. Valerie, a professional caregiver herself, was caring for her father who had recently been hospitalized for heart failure and a stroke:

> We couldn't get the right foods for Father at the medical center. He was supposed to get soft foods and they brought him pork chops! The attitude of the employees at the hospital was sloppy and indifferent. One department didn't care what the other was doing. They never looked at Father as a person.
>
> Father's doctor met me in the hall one day. He wanted to discharge him and asked me if I thought he could take his own medicine. Father was weak, incoherent, and blind! The doctor never even looked at him; he only consulted the charts! I pitched a fit right there in the hall.

One of the informal caregivers' most frequent complaints involved professionals who were sometimes unresponsive. Numerous participants in our study cited examples of health-care or social service personnel ignoring their input or failing to inform them of treatment protocols. Cassie said, "They shouldn't be so damned professional. Nobody wants a starchy person when they're distressed." June's response typified many:

> The physicians don't talk to me, don't give me information I can relate to, don't listen to my concerns or ideas, like the fact that I believe that emotional and physical issues are both important. I would like for them to be more open to me and to spend more time telling me the side effects of medications

or how I can deal with my daughter better. For example, when I called for the results of a test, the only information I was given was that the "prognosis is poor." They never told me what I should expect or what to do about it.

Matt, the father of a child suffering from severe cerebral palsy, described the feelings of some participants best when he said, "The professional caregivers should accept that lay caregivers are the 'professionals' in this specific situation. They know more about the individual than anyone else. They shouldn't prejudge the caregiver because of his social/economic/cultural/racial/religious background. They should *listen to the caregiver.*"

On behalf of the formal caregivers whom we interviewed, I must say that most were pained by the lack of time they had to minister to their patients and family members. Many complained of spending half their lives doing administrative tasks and paperwork. Funding cutbacks in government programs also meant that fewer professionals were caring for more individuals. As one formal caregiver put it, "So many clients, not enough you."

Although the informal caregivers had many complaints, I don't want you to come away with the impression that they found their activities unrewarding. Our study revealed that 88 percent of the participants found caregiving a gratifying and worthwhile endeavor.

Some, like Mildred, who was caring for her aged mother, derived great pride in the preservation of their loved one's security and dignity. "My caregiving makes a difference to me," Mildred explained. "I know I'm doing what my mother would do for herself. She has always been a 'Southern lady,' prim and proper. I assure that she is clean, well cared for, and that her needs are met. She's treated with dignity and respect."

Many lay caregivers spoke of positive changes in their attitudes and quality of life as a result of their activities. Quite a few said that now they had more empathy and compassion, more patience, less frustration, and more respect for caregivers and those needing care. Others learned coping skills and the art of self-preservation. Mildred put it well when she said, "I've learned you can't have everything you want. You have to accept things in life that are given to you. You learn patience and to be thankful."

And a few family caregivers spoke of how their loved one's struggle led them to be advocates for others suffering from the same illness and for other caregivers. Alice had been encouraged to institutionalize her severely disabled son at birth. She and her husband chose not to. "Prior to Kenny's birth," she explained, "I was quiet, shy, and polite. Now I'm an advocate— a fighter for the rights of all people, but especially the disabled."

Jerry established a grief support group in his town after his young son died of a rare ailment. And Walter became involved in the local American Cancer Society chapter. "I spend time in the ACS office," he said, "making packets for others who need information. I'm on the board of directors and am a speaker for the organization."

Many of the caregivers found the greatest rewards when their loved ones made progress, even in some small way. They cherished the special moments that transcended the daily pain. Joan, nurturing a stepdaughter who suffers from schizophrenia, enjoyed the fact that "Sharon has such a beautiful voice and wants to sing all the time." And Alice took great pleasure in significant turning points: when her son, Kenny, learned to communicate with the family and welcomed her home for the first time; when he mastered eating with a spoon.

And for many caregivers, the greatest moments occur when their loved ones express gratitude and affection. "Recently," explained Ruth, "my mother looked at me and thanked me for what I had done." This she classified as her best caregiving experience. And Marsha derived enormous joy from the moments that her mentally ill son put his arms around her neck and hugged her.

LOOKING TO THE FUTURE

As a result of our study, the research team made recommendations that would help remedy problems raised by caregivers during the interviews. The CARE-NET Leadership Council has already acted upon some of these suggestions, including the establishment of training programs, peer support groups, and a resource center in our region. I'll cover these issues more fully in Chapter 7, but wouldn't it be wonderful if there were a CARE-NET in communities all across our country so that people who do need help could get it?

4.

&DUCATE AND PREPARE YOURSELF

"Somebody needs to give caregivers a road map!" That's what one participant in our study said, and I'm sure his statement echoes the sentiments of many.

It's natural to feel bewildered by it all. Most caregivers do. Most have never before faced the situations they now find themselves in. I frequently receive letters from family caregivers appealing to me for help. "We don't know where to go or what to do," they write. "We've exhausted all of our financial resources, and we're frightened."

Many don't have the information they need to cope successfully with the illness they are suddenly forced to deal with. "What do the symptoms mean?" "Why won't the medicine work?" Others have difficulty envisioning the future. "What can I expect?" they ask. "How should I make arrangements? Is my insurance or Medicare going to pay?"

Indeed, informal caregivers in our CARE-NET study named "specialized training" and "information" among their top ten needs. When asked during his interview what resources he found indispensable, one family caregiver said, "a caring consultant" to help him work through the complex service-delivery system, especially in the early stages of his caregiving. Another said, "We need a pipeline for caregivers to go to for help and information." And a third added, "The lack of information and difficulties with insurance and accessing the system can enhance helplessness, hopelessness, and despair."

In this book I spend a lot of time discussing the emotional and psychological aspects of caregiving. But what might confront you first when you become a caregiver—a situation that can develop quickly, even overnight—is the sheer number of overwhelming, nuts-and-bolts details of the job. Where do you start? Here I will present some strategies—a caregivers' road map of sorts—that may relieve those feelings of helplessness, hopelessness, and despair. By educating and preparing yourself, you can improve your ability to carry out your caregiving role. The more information you have, the more comfortable you'll be making important decisions. There are people who can and will help you, if only you know whom to ask.

EDUCATE YOURSELF

Throughout this book, I'll suggest how to learn all you can about your loved one's illness. Let me provide a thumbnail sketch of the many ways to gather information. I'll discuss many of these in greater depth in the chapters to follow.

Ask your loved one's professional care providers. Ask to sit in on diagnosis and treatment discussions with your loved one's physicians and other members of the health-care team. Introduce yourself as the caregiver and inquire about the disease's course and treatment and about possible side effects of the medications. Bring written questions and take notes or tape-record the session. If you have too many concerns to be answered in ten or fifteen minutes, schedule a separate consultation.

Ask the professionals to recommend books or give you handouts and brochures on the condition. Inquire about peer support groups or other helpful resources or national organizations. (Chapter 9 has more information on dealing with your ill family member's formal caregivers.)

Consult a private clinical social worker or gerontologist. These individuals are trained to navigate the complex health-care delivery network. They can come into your home, assess your family's needs, and then help you locate a home-care program, a physical therapist, a day-care center, a household helper, or even a mechanized bed. They may have investigated nursing homes in your community and be able to help you decide which is best for your needs. They understand the rules governing Medicare and Medicaid and can advise you about what to expect from the system.

You can hire social workers to make weekly or monthly visits to your home. Or you can employ them one time only, to help you reorganize your household during the adjustment phase. They are usually paid an hourly fee for their services. Some insurance plans reimburse you for these counseling fees.

Use a support group.

There are support groups for most problems. People who are dealing with the same situation that you are now facing can offer practical assistance about lift equipment, tube feedings, wound care, and other needs. Their wisdom is garnered from years of hard-earned experience. If you're living in a small town, you may have to start your own support network. See Chapter 7 and Appendix B for suggestions on where to find groups or, if none exists, how to create your own.

Contact a national organization. Appendix B has a listing of national organizations dealing with specific diseases. These groups often have written materials explaining the ailment and can offer varying degrees of support—some even sponsor support groups. If you can't find an organization covering your loved one's illness in Appendix B, check with the self-help clearinghouses listed. Your phone book can be a useful tool. You might also try calling 1-800-555-1212. This is the national toll-free 800-number information line. Assuming the organization you need has a toll-free number, the operator may assist you in locating it.

Check with your hospital. Many hospitals have programs such as a "stroke club" or a "heart families" group. Some even have groups for organ transplant patients. If your institution doesn't offer such a program, ask the head nurse or social worker about getting one started. If that's impossible, inquire about programs at other hospitals or in neighboring towns.

Nurses and social workers are good resources for information about home care. They can help you arrange for in-home nursing services. Hospitals may also offer seminars on home care to inpatients who are about to be discharged and the family members who will be caring for them. Certified diabetes educators and registered nutritionists might also be helpful. With patients leaving hospitals earlier and earlier these days, it's wise to get as much information as you can before the ill one comes home.

Use hotlines. The federal government and private organizations have hotlines that provide information about particular diseases. Others, such as suicide-prevention hotlines, offer crisis intervention. You will find some hotlines listed in Appendix B. The 800-number information operator can assist you in finding others not listed here.

Do some research. Visit the local library or bookstore. Many general-interest books have been published about the most common diseases. You may find first-person accounts written by patients or their family members as well as strictly informational guides authored by professionals but meant for the lay person. (There is a representative collection of books listed in Appendix B.) If the disease you are trying to learn about is a rare ailment, you can probably find books on the subject at a hospital or university library. These, of course, might be somewhat more technical.

You can always ask another physician for more information and a second opinion. In Chapter 9, I explain how to do so.

You might also want to investigate whether scientists are conducting research into the particular illness. If so, your family member may want to become involved in a "clinical trial" as a final lifesaving measure. We did that for Jimmy's brother, Billy. He went to the National Cancer Institute for treatment. If the decision is made to become involved in such an experimental program, all services should be free.

Ask your physicians about who is doing the research within your area. If they have no information, contact the National Institutes of Health in Bethesda, Maryland, to learn about government-funded research. Often, participants in these studies must meet strict prerequisites to qualify, so be patient and realistic.

PLAN FOR A CRISIS

The worst time to make a decision is when you're upset and anxious about a downturn in your ill one's health—or your own. You may feel confused and distracted, or be unable to concentrate to the point that you don't understand what professionals are telling you. It is far better to make plans in advance for the kinds of situations you may face later on. But it is also human nature to avoid bringing up these issues. They are things we don't want to think about and wish would never occur.

Still, superstitions aside, thinking and talking about something doesn't make it happen any sooner. Here are some questions you might consider:

Will I be able to provide all the care my ill family member needs? You've just taken on what could be a full-time job. Who can you count on when you need assistance? Can someone offer respite? Ask a friend or a family member to act as a backup in case you are suddenly unavailable. A family meeting would be advisable to deal with this issue (see Chapter 6).

One of my colleagues recently faced such a dilemma when both elderly parents became ill at the same time. Could you cope with such an eventuality? If not, make plans with your family about how to organize others to help. To be sure everyone understands and agrees to his or her responsibilities, write down the emergency plan and mail it to all involved.

Have I left contingency instructions? Do you know who will call the doctor or an ambulance if you are unreachable at work when an emergency arises? You might need a concrete plan for such issues.

Leave a list of important phone numbers, including those of the doctor, the hospital, and a trusted family member or your backup with your loved one or with a sitter, if it's necessary to hire one. If there is some question about how to proceed, provide instructions on how to reach your backup. If it's a life-and-death situation, the sitter should dial 911 *first*—then call you and the family backup for support.

You might also want to duplicate and share the list of vital information (such as social security numbers, insurance policies, and medical records), below, with others in your family or with your backup. Include instructions about the timing and dosage of medications, dietary restrictions, and/or other activities that you may perform automatically but that others would have no way of knowing about.

Do I have all the information I will need? Legal experts advise you to gather basic information to have on hand. These include your disabled family member's:

- insurance policies for health care, disability, life, nursing-home care, home or apartment (fire, theft, and liability), and cars
- social security number
- account numbers and institutions for savings and checking

accounts, stocks and bonds, and profit-sharing and retirement pensions
- safe-deposit box location and key
- legal description of real estate property (as is found on a property tax bill) or other assets and debts
- medical records including comprehensive lists of doctors, prescriptions, and drug allergies or other harmful reactions to treatment
- the location of a will, a living will, and a durable power of attorney for health decisions (see below), if they have been signed. (The only copy should never be kept in a safe-deposit box in case the key can't be located in an emergency.)

Does my ill family member have a will? Individuals must be "of sound mind" when they draw up wills. It is therefore imperative that disabled family members see to this piece of business before they lose the capacity to make important decisions. For example, those diagnosed with Alzheimer's or Parkinson's disease (which in some cases can also lead to dementia) should have their wills drawn up as early as possible in the course of their illness, while they are still lucid. The best wills are written with the assistance of a competent attorney.

Does my loved one have a "living will"? A living will (also called a "directive to physicians" or a "declaration as to treatment") instructs treating and consulting physicians to withhold or cease any life-prolonging measures when one is terminally ill and the professionals have determined that there is no medical probability for recovery. It indicates the desire to die naturally, with only pain medication to keep one as comfortable as possible. If unable to give consent for withholding treatment at the moment of crisis, the ill one may also designate in the living will someone who can give the consent. Typically, it takes effect when the ill one becomes incapacitated and unable to communicate his or her wishes. This document is not only for ill or disabled individuals. Jimmy and I both have recently signed our own.

If the one you are caring for has a living will, several people need copies. These include the primary and secondary physicians, family members, and certainly the individual designated to make the final decision, should the need arise. If you are that person, you may feel relieved to have the document stating your loved one's wishes at that delicate moment.

What if my ill family member becomes incapacitated?   Your family member should sign a *durable power of attorney*, allowing someone else (an "agent" or "attorney-in-fact")—most likely, you—to have permanent access to bank accounts and make important property-related and financial decisions in the event he or she cannot make these because of incapacitation. Such an agreement should be signed *before* it is actually needed and will go into effect when the crisis occurs. The one signing can specify how much or how little control to give the attorney-in-fact and can cancel the agreement at any time.

This document is relatively easy and inexpensive to create. Preprinted forms are even available in stationery stores. It may require notarization, however, and your family member must be mentally competent in order to sign it.

In a *durable power of attorney for health decisions,* your loved one specifies who should act on his or her behalf in medical matters in the event of incapacitation. In it, an individual can state his or her wishes regarding medical treatment, including feeding or hydration decisions, the use of life-sustaining technology, and admission and discharge from the hospital. However, unlike a living will, this document is not reserved only for those who are terminally ill. It can also be used for any condition, including comas. Standard forms are obtainable from most health-care providers and usually must be witnessed and notarized.

Guardianship, also called *conservatorship,* is a more drastic measure in which the court declares individuals incompetent and appoints others ("guardians" or "conservators") to take charge of their property and personal well-being. This is an all-or-nothing measure—either an individual is competent or not—and it can create harsh feelings among family members. The court may appoint two individuals—one as a guardian of the person and the other as a guardian of the property—and sometimes they don't agree on how to care for the incapacitated loved one. You would be wise to consult an attorney if you wish to deal with your situation in this way.

Who will provide care if I am no longer able to? Do I have a will? For everyone's peace of mind, be sure to have a family discussion and a plan in place before the need arises. Many of the caregivers in our study were most apprehensive about this possibility.

A will can help you feel more at ease by delineating how you would like your assets divided and how your disabled one will be cared for in your absence. But attorneys recommend that the wills of caregivers be slightly different from those of other individuals.

Most people leave all of their assets directly to spouses, or if their spouses have died, to the children. However, if surviving individuals are mentally incompetent or otherwise unable to manage their own affairs, the court will appoint a conservator who may or may not carry out the deceased one's wishes. It is better to have the inheritance placed in a *discretionary trust* and name the *trustee(s)*—the individual(s) who will make the decisions regarding care for your loved one. You can specify how you wish the ill family member to be cared for in the discretionary trust.

If you are the guardian, include in your will the name of the individual you want to take over your caregiving role upon your death or incapacitation. (Be sure to discuss your decision with this person first.) It's also wise to name an alternate guardian, in case your first choice has died or is otherwise unable to take over these duties.

Living trusts are complex financial arrangements for individuals with relatively large estates. Wills and living wills can be included as part of a living trust.

These are all complicated issues with far-reaching consequences. A discussion with a lawyer specializing in wills and trusts is advisable.

Do I need a life insurance policy? If you're employed outside the home, your disabled family member may depend on your income for care. Your sudden death might leave the loved one impoverished and vulnerable. But even if you're a full-time caregiver, and don't earn an outside income, the services you provide for free would cost a good deal of money for those taking over the care.

It is wise, therefore, for caregivers to have life insurance policies. Experts advise that a standard term policy is the simplest option, and often it's quite sufficient. The funds should be placed in a discretionary trust upon your death. Consult a reputable insurance agent or attorney for the best choice in your situation.

How does my loved one feel about nursing-home placement? Explore with your family member under what circumstances such placement would be acceptable. To eliminate the element of surprise and the resentment that might accompany it, discuss this issue and shop for a facility together before it is actually needed. I'll share some important information on this topic in Chapter 10.

Have I made arrangements with my employer? According to a recent *Wall Street Journal* article, approximately 22 percent of the workforce expects to take over caregiving responsibilities by the year 1997. That is up from 15 percent in 1994. And the number may grow to 37 percent by 2005.

Employees and their supervisors are often unprepared for the disruptions that caregiving can bring. The Family Leave Act protects one's job during an absence of several months per year to care for a family member. But what if your caregiving duties exceed the limit?

Discuss with your boss the possibility of a flexible schedule. You might experiment with working at home several days a week (using a computer modem and fax to stay in touch with your company) or sharing a full-time position with another colleague (job sharing).

Some companies have been forward-looking in offering their employees elder-care planning seminars and referrals to attorneys and social workers to help navigate the Medicare and health-delivery system. They understand that their workers are more productive when they are not burdened with excessive worries and family caregiving dilemmas. As one benefits manager explained to the *Wall Street Journal* reporter, "We'd be a little foolhardy not to recognize that caregivers need support." Hopefully, your employer will be equally enlightened.

Do I have an attorney who can help with these complex decisions and arrangements? The old adage "An ounce of prevention is worth a pound of cure" applies in this case. Find a competent attorney in your community. Your friends or employer can give you recommendations. You can also look in the telephone book for the Better Business Bureau to ask for information.

The National Academy of Elder Law Attorneys and the American Bar Association Commission on Legal Problems of the Elderly can refer you to lawyers in your area who specialize in problems associated with illness, incapacitation, and aging. The phone numbers of these organizations are listed in Appendix B.

Again, I realize how difficult it may be for you even to think about the harsh and perhaps frightening realities that lurk behind making a will, buying life insurance, or thinking about death. I can tell you from experience, however, that learning all you can about a loved one's illness and preparing to the best of your abilities for any crises that might arise will bring you peace of mind. Taking care of these one-time details will help you to take the measure of your caregiving role and organize your life for the challenge that lies ahead. I hope it will also bring you a sense of control over your situation—and that in itself can be a tremendous comfort.

5.

*Y*OUR EMOTIONAL DILEMMAS AS A FAMILY CAREGIVER

When a family member becomes ill, the whole family suffers. While they have been spared the physical or mental symptoms of the ailment, the other members are also affected. I can vouch for that from my own family's experience.

Even though it was years ago, my mother still talks about being nervous all the time when my father was sick and couldn't seem to get better. Then, having the doctor tell her that Daddy wouldn't live devastated her. She had been so worried, so afraid that the worst was going to happen—and then it did. All of a sudden, she had to shoulder the burden alone of raising four small children, running the household, tending the finances, and at the same time caring for her terminally ill husband. But as my mother used to say, "When you find out that the one you love is not going to be able to live, he's the one you care about, not yourself."

I suffered too during my father's illness and after his and my grandmother's deaths. During that time and for some years after, I was a very unhappy young person.

Before Daddy's diagnosis, I had always been conscientious about my schoolwork and had been rewarded for my efforts with straight A's and school prizes. But once he became ill, I didn't care about anything else but him. I didn't want to study. I would take my books into his room and sit on the floor next to his bed, but it was no use. I couldn't concentrate. I remember going to school one day and admitting to my teacher, Miss Julia Coleman, that I didn't have my lessons—for the first time in my life.

I had had some bad feelings about my father before he got sick—as I think all children do at times—especially after he disciplined me. Because he was strict and demanding, I sometimes thought he was mean and didn't love me. But once he became sick, I thought that if I had been good, if I had never had any of these negative thoughts, then maybe this terrible illness would not have happened. Secretly I felt totally responsible for his disease.

I prayed for his recovery, to no avail. Before, I had had faith that I could achieve anything I set out to do. But with his worsening condition and eventual death, I lost all confidence. After all, my prayers couldn't keep my father alive. I began questioning whether God loved me, and then I felt guilty about having those thoughts.

After Daddy and my grandmother died, I felt sorry for myself and wondered why these things were happening to me. Not only that, I was afraid that something was going to happen to my mother. I worried about her constantly. Then, at the age of nineteen, I married Jimmy and immediately left home to join him at his naval post. I was gone for seven years. I left my mother with three small children to raise and my grandfather to care for. I felt guilty about that for many years, too.

I didn't tell anyone about these guilty feelings, especially not my mother. I didn't want to add to her burden with my worries. So the emotions remained buried within me for decades and only emerged when I finally explored them in my autobiography.

YOUR COMPLEX EMOTIONS

These events of my childhood affected me and my family profoundly. And like me, you may be experiencing many emotions that are difficult to manage.

You may feel great sadness that your child is unlike other children—unable to run and play, ride a bike, or go to school. Or you may endure a sense of loss when your wife, whom you love dearly, can no longer do what she was once able to do— when she is incapable of going out to a movie or a restaurant, or when she has lost the ability to read or speak or work. The friend, companion, lover, and partner that you once enjoyed may now be only a shadow of her former self, and you may experience that loss deeply.

You may also be frightened. If the progress of your family member's illness is erratic, you are constantly under the stress of not knowing what to expect. One day your son seems fine, the next day he is incapacitated again. You may find it difficult to plan for the future, or even for daily activities. Your anxiety and helplessness in the face of your son's deteriorating condition may be painful beyond measure.

If the one you are caring for contributed significantly to your household income, you may also fear the financial repercussions of that lack of ability to work. This, of course, comes in addition to medical and long-term nursing-care costs, some (or many) of which are not covered by Medicare or private insurance. You may feel humiliated at having to ask others, even the government, for financial assistance.

And the deepest anxiety of all, if your family member suffers from a terminal illness, is that of the impending death. How will you live without the one you love so much?

As I did, maybe you also feel debilitating guilt about the situation. You believe you were somehow responsible for the illness or worry that you're not doing enough to help the suffering one, even though you're already at the end of your rope. Or you feel guilty for the resentment you're experiencing. Like me, you may believe that God is punishing you for former transgressions, or you might even lose faith in God for having made a good and innocent person suffer so much. Guilt such as this may interfere with your energy and your ability to be helpful.

Also, as did some of the respondents to our CARE-NET study, you may feel ambivalent, resentful, angry, trapped, and burdened. Perhaps your family member is ungrateful or physically or emotionally unable to express gratitude. How you long to hear those sweet words, "Thank you." You are sometimes enraged that recalcitrant family members are unwilling to help you. You may wonder when there will be time for your needs, or why, when friends and relatives inquire about your ill one's condition, they never ask how you are doing. You could certainly use a shoulder to cry on from time to time too. You are lonely and sometimes even jealous of the attention your family member is receiving, then guilty for having these thoughts. And you're exhausted.

All of these reactions are normal and to be expected. After all, it's unlikely that your loved one's illness would engender happy emotions! Many caregivers experience these feelings every day of their lives. Some psychologists advise that feelings are neither right nor wrong, neither good nor bad. Feelings don't always have to make sense. In order for you to do the best job possible for the one who is ill, it is important for you to acknowledge your emotions, if only to yourself. Feel your pain and grieve your losses if you must. Whether you like or understand them, these emotions are real and deserve your attention. They give you valuable information about yourself.

But you should also remember that most negative periods are transitory. They come and go. If you are feeling sad and frightened or angry and resentful today, tomorrow you may have a new lease on life. A friend drops by with a bouquet of flowers just for you, or your loved one squeezes your hand and whispers, "I love you," and you feel ready to go on, at least for one more day.

In this chapter, I would like to explore with you some of the emotional dilemmas you might be facing as a family caregiver. By delineating them, maybe I can provide you with some tools to deal with them.

THE ILL ONE'S EXPERIENCE

Even as you are struggling with your own problems and feelings, you may find that the one you are caring for seems moody, withdrawn, depressed, or perhaps—even more unsettling—unnaturally cheerful. It can help you to cope with your position if you have a better understanding of what your loved one is experiencing.

People facing chronic illness suffer great emotional turmoil. The prospect of being sick and a burden to someone else, possibly of facing death, can be devastating.

I witnessed my father's suffering when he learned that he had leukemia and would not live. Most of all, he worried about my mother and what would become of us children. One day he called us into his room, and with tears in his eyes, said that the time had come to tell us that he couldn't get well. "You are good children," he said, "and you're going to have to take care of Mother for me." He talked for a long time that day, telling us about his dreams for our future. He wanted us to go to college and have opportunities he never had. He told my mother to sell even the farm if she needed the money for our education. His greatest sorrow, he said, was that he was not going to be there to make sure we all got a good education and had good lives.

In their book, *Taking Charge: Overcoming the Challenges of Long-Term Illness,* Irene Pollin, a clinical social worker who specializes in helping chronically ill individuals and their families, and my coauthor, Susan K. Golant, delineate eight fears that people coping with chronic illness usually face. These are borne out by my own experience with my father and by the experiences of the respondents in the RCI survey:

1. *The fear of loss of control.* Your family member may fear that he has lost control over his life because of his illness. Like my father, he may have made plans for the future, which are now put into question. He doesn't know from one day to the next how he will feel or whether he will ever be able to regain control of his life.

2. *The fear of changed self-image.* Sometimes the one who is ill no longer views herself as the same person. She feels less confident, no longer attractive, physically weaker, and somehow damaged. Maybe she has lost her fertility or her gracefulness, her ability to earn a living or her willingness to believe in God, and sees herself as defective and unlovable.

3. *The fear of dependency.* My father was the oldest son in his family. When he was twenty, his father died and Daddy became the head of their household, caring for five brothers and a sister before he married and had his own family. He had always been strong and tough, the one who shouldered the responsibility. But as a result of his illness he became the dependent one.

Once the reality of the illness has settled in and the one you are caring for recognizes that her condition is not going away, she, too, may fear her loss of independence. Hating to show any vulnerability, she may have difficulty accepting outside help, or, giving in to her fears, she may become overly needy and dependent on you. One of the respondents in our CARE-NET study told us that it was becoming more and more difficult for her to care for her chronically ill daughter because the daughter expected everything to be done for her. She is "totally spoiled," the mother said.

4. *The fear of stigma.* Another of the respondents commented, "I share some with friends, but friends 'pull back' due to the illness."

The one you are caring for may become frightened that others will distance themselves from him once they know he is sick, as if illness brought with it some sort of shame. If he is disfigured in some way or if the illness causes some apparent physical disability—an uneven gait, a drooping lip, a useless arm—he could be afraid that others will point and stare, causing him to withdraw into the confines of home.

5. *The fear of abandonment.* As a natural part of infancy, babies fear that their parents won't be available or loving when they need them. They cry when parents leave the room. These feelings stay within us and actually become intensified with an illness. Even if yours is the most affectionate and giving of families, your ill family member may grow frightened that you will tire of the drudgery that the constant care involves. This normal and universal anxiety stems from the disease threatening his personal sense of security.

6. *The fear of expressing anger.* When those suffering realize that they have done everything possible, yet can "never" be cured of their disease, they may become intensely angry. It's easy to see how a chronic condition could give rise to lots of anger. Anger is a consequence of frustration. Yet many people are afraid to express anger because they have been taught that this is an unacceptable emotion or because they're afraid of driving others away with their rage. Or they're afraid of flying out of control. But from my years of experience working in the field of mental health, I know that anger kept inside can cause depression and a lack of energy.

7. *The fear of isolation.* Physical, social, and emotional isolation can result from a chronic illness. Ill ones, physically confined, lose the opportunity to socialize with old friends and often find themselves withdrawing further from them. The fear of isolation usually doesn't occur immediately after their diagnosis. It takes time for ill ones to pull away from society or to recognize that friends, family, acquaintances, and co-workers are avoiding them.

8. *The fear of death.* Although everyone who is diagnosed with a serious chronic illness fears death, Irene Pollin, who has experience working with chronically ill people and their families, says that, ironically, death is usually not what they fear the most. Rather, their greatest fears revolve around how they will live with the illness until they die.

YOUR EXPERIENCE

Perhaps this list has made you feel guilty. "How can I complain," you may be thinking. "I'm not the sick one. Look at what the one I'm caring for is going through." And if this illness is terminal, you may add, "When this is all over, I'll still be alive and well. What right have I to feel sorry for myself?"

The fact is, even if you are well, you still have been dealt a fate you neither wanted nor deserved. Being a family caregiver is a tough job, one that requires patience, forbearance, physical and emotional stamina, and an iron will. It can alter your life's course.

As the disabled family member goes through these fears, you, the caregiver, experience them too, but in your own way.

To illustrate, I'd like to share with you a portion of Jerry Wise's story.

Jerry is a man in his mid-forties living in the neighboring town of Americus. Several years ago, he lost his young son to a rare and incurable malady. Through tears of pain, he told us about his experiences at the Fourth Annual Conference of the Rosalynn Carter Institute.

I was married with three children. We had a very normal family until one afternoon in late September, 1980, when the bottom of our world fell out.

Something wasn't right with our youngest child, who was seventeen months old. After many tests, the doctor came into his office where my wife and I were waiting and said, "Your son has been diagnosed with the infantile form of Lou Gehrig's disease. There's no cure. There's nothing that can be done. I'm letting you take him home tonight. And if he's alive when you get him home, you just love him as long as you have him, because it won't be long."

If you haven't been there, there's no way to understand the stress, the emotions, the grief that ensues as a result of such a statement. It changed our lives forever. I'll never be the same person again.

But God was gracious to us and allowed us to keep that young fella for almost twelve years. The doctors missed the prognosis. They did not miss the diagnosis as much as we denied it and denied it and denied it. We went through ten years and three months of continuous anxiety, not knowing whether we'd wake up the next morning and he'd be there with us, alive.

The emotions are indescribable; the support, nonexistent. It's not because people didn't care, it's not because people didn't want to help us. People didn't know what to do. Our own family members didn't want to talk about it, didn't want to hear about it. Our friends were uncomfortable with it. We were isolated.

For the first three years (after the initial shock of the diagnosis wore off), it was pretty easy to deny the disease. Everything went fine. He was, from all outward appearances, a normal little boy, other than the fact that he could not walk. He was confined to a wheelchair. I carried him most everywhere to keep the stigma of the wheelchair away. He was a little fella, and I could tote him, no problem. But sometimes, we'd walk through a mall and people would say, "Why don't you put that big boy down and let him walk?" Little did they know, if I put him down, he just sat there.

At the age of five, came the first real obstacle for us. Our son developed pneumonia. The doctor said, "This is it. His respiratory function is very weak. He will not be able to survive this."

Our son was a fighter. He came through as any normal child would. But the stress and strain and anxiety for three years coupled with those ten days of intense hospitalization (during which my wife never left his bedside) took a toll on my wife.

We got home from the hospital about noon one day. By the middle of the afternoon, she had a complete emotional breakdown. For the next five years, she had to fight severe depression.

And so I had two older children who were perfectly normal in every sense of the word, who had normal lives that we had to be able to maintain; I had a wife who was emotionally depleted; and I had a son who was terminally ill. We had a lot of caring people, loving people, but very, very little support.

I'll have more to say about Jerry in Chapter 11, because he is one of those remarkable people who are able to transform their tragedies into help for others. But, as you can see from his story, although Jerry was a caregiver and not sick himself, he, too, experienced many of the same fears and emotions that an individual diagnosed with a long-term illness would. His son's disease affected him and the rest of his family deeply.

To understand your own feelings, ask yourself the following questions:

- Do I feel as if my life is now spinning out of my control?
- Do I feel as if I'm a different person since my family member was diagnosed?
- Do I resent that my previously independent loved one has now become dependent on me?
- Am I afraid that others will make derogatory comments about my ill one's appearance or condition? Does this keep me from going out more often?
- Do I sometimes wish that I could run away from my situation?
- Do I feel angry:
    —At my family member for constantly needing my attention?
    —At myself for my own limitations?
    —At others for their insensitivity or unwillingness to help?
    —At the illness itself?
- Have I lost connections with friends and family? Do I feel isolated and alone?
- Do I worry about the impending death of the one I love? Do I sometimes look forward to it with a sense of relief?

If you answered yes to any or all of these, do not feel ashamed. These are normal responses for a person in a caregiving role. Now let's see what you can do to ease your feelings.

GRIEVING YOUR LOSSES

You may find it useful to list and grieve the losses you experience as a caregiver. These can be mundane, such as lost income or vacation or weekly bridge games or quiet talks with your husband at the beach. They can be more abstract and all-encompassing, such as lost freedom, privacy, mothering, companionship, or sexuality. Sometimes anticipatory mourning can go on for many months or years. You bemoan the losses of the ability to function one by one: when your loved one can no longer drive, can no longer walk, can no longer recognize you.

If, after noting all that you and the one you care for have lost, you feel like crying, let the tears flow. You're entitled. In fact, Los Angeles psychologist Dr. Leonard Felder recommends a weekly cry. "Just like heavy rainfall clears the air and is followed by the sweet sound of birds singing," he writes in his book, *When a Loved One Is Ill*, "so does a good cry bathe your insides with a healing release." Dr. Felder encourages caregivers to cry perhaps by watching sad movies, or while taking hot showers, looking at photos of their loved one, or going on long walks near a body of water.

Crying is a valuable way to release pain, frustration, anger, and grief. As Karen Ring, a licensed clinical social worker, explains in a chapter on caring and grieving published in the *Florida Caregivers Handbook*, "Grief can reaffirm or destroy the very foundation of our spiritual beliefs about what life is and what it means to us. Finding meaning in the experience of loss is a key in the grieving process."

OTHER WAYS YOU CAN HELP YOURSELF

The following suggestions may also help you to come to grips with the issues you are facing. Keep in mind that at times you may not be able to change your situation, but you can change the way you think about it.

I feel as if my life is spinning out of control. You may feel as if your life's course is now dictated by the whims of your dependent one's illness. This is truly frightening. To better cope, try taking charge of what you can control. Try to carve out some time every day that is yours and yours alone. It might make you feel better to weed a small patch in your garden or work a crossword puzzle. Find ways to reduce your stress. An afternoon at the movies with a friend, or a walk around the block if you can get away for a few minutes, or even making yourself a simple cup of tea just the way you like it can restore your energy and sense of control, at least for the moment.

It may also help to pay attention to those occasions when you feel as if you've done all you can do. In preparing this chapter, I asked Jimmy if he had felt helpless and out of control during those difficult years when his sisters and brother were dying of cancer. He replied that he had not. He had worked hard to do what he could; he researched clinical trials of new experimental drugs and helped his family benefit any way he knew how. When he had exhausted all the available resources, then he accepted the fact that there was nothing else to be done. This gave him some sense of peace.

Ask yourself: What more can I do after I've done all I can? Allow yourself the peace of mind that comes from extending yourself as fully as you know how.

I feel as if I'm a different person than I was before the illness. This may be true. It is possible that the illness has altered your life as well as that of your loved one. And while you might resent some of the unwelcome changes such as constant exhaustion and anxiety or changed life plans, it is helpful to recognize that you may have grown from this experience, also.

Like many caregivers in our CARE-NET study, you might notice that you have become more compassionate and patient as a result of your family member's illness. You may be less likely to take things for granted and gain a greater appreciation for what you still have, in spite of your losses. You probably will also find that you have strength you never knew you possessed. You can take pride in being the family's sole breadwinner now, or in your newfound nursing expertise. Many of our CARE-NET participants expressed pleasure in maintaining their loved one's dignity over the course of the illness. The illness may have changed you, but perhaps some of these changes are for the better.

I resent my loved one's dependence. This can be a tricky issue. As you will see in the next chapter, many who are ill become totally dependent on their caregivers while others refuse to give up their independence, even if it's damaging for them not to do so.

Do bear in mind, however, that in some instances, caregivers, in their need to protect the one they are caring for, may become overly solicitous. They may refuse to allow others to provide respite or interfere when they do, or they may step in too often and usurp what little power the ill one still possesses.

You can take away a person's self-worth or sense of the importance of life if you do everything and take total control. Allow your family member as much independence as possible. Let go a little bit, even if you think you can accomplish a task better, even if it is painful for you to watch the disabled one struggle to do things alone.

One of my friends, Margie, told me about watching her husband try to do some work in the yard. He had had a very serious heart attack and was having a problem with circulation in his leg. The doctor told him that he must move around, not sit or stand for long periods of time. "But I couldn't make him get up out of that chair," Margie said, "and one day I just really fussed at him, and then I went out where he couldn't see me and cried and cried." But her husband got up and walked a little!

After that, he began to try to take take care of the yard work. Margie said he could only work for a few minutes, then he would have to rest, but he would keep at it until he finished the job—all the time complaining about how long it was taking him and how hard it was! "It hurt me to watch him, and I felt so guilty. I could have done the job for him in half the time, and he wouldn't have had to worry about it. But," she continued, "at the end of the day, he would look back and be so proud of what he had been able to accomplish."

It upsets me when others point and stare at us. It is part of human nature to feel threatened or curious about those who are "different" among us. We are all frightened by our vulnerability and mortality. It is reasonable to expect that people will stop and stare if one is disfigured or disabled in some way. Jerry Wise tried to protect his son from this response by carrying him wherever they went instead of using a wheelchair, but still people made unkind remarks.

Unfortunately, if you allow your fear of stigma to control your behavior, you may find yourself becoming more and more isolated. You may shun old friends, give up activities you once enjoyed, and just forget how to have fun. Although it's difficult, it's better to wear the disability as a badge of courage rather than a source of shame.

Choose with whom and how you share news of the illness. It might be easier to explain it to strangers at first rather than to friends, because you have less invested in their response. Don't take slights or gaping stares personally. If you feel that you or your loved one is actively being discriminated against, take action. The organizations listed in Appendix B may help you deal with this dilemma.

I feel like running away from home! If you're feeling overwhelmed by your caregiving responsibilities, you may be experiencing burnout. See Chapter 8 for the signs of burnout and strategies to help you cope with this problem—or, hopefully, to avoid it.

I'm really angry. As frustration and anger can be natural consequences of chronic illnesses, by association, they can be consequences of your caregiving. You are caught in a position you never wanted to be in. It's perfectly normal to feel angry. But bear in mind that you're angry at the illness, not necessarily at the one you are caring for.

Be careful how you express your anger. Glowering, stomping around the house, or behaving in a hostile way are rarely effective. And while it's normal to have arguments from time to time, there is little to gain from blasting the ill one with months and months of pent-up rage. Your family member may be as frustrated and angry as you are. And both of you may feel hurt and guilty after you've had an explosive encounter. It is also possible that, because of his or her condition, your loved one may be incapable of dealing with or understanding your feelings.

You may need to vent your anger elsewhere. You might find it helpful to go out to your car, turn your stereo up too high, and scream as loud as you can. One of the best things to do, which is also healthy, is to take some exercise. Walk briskly, jog, buy a videotape and do some aerobics, or maybe jump rope. You might even try lifting weights. Exercise will serve more than one purpose. It will strengthen you, which is important if you have to help physically with the one you are caring for, and will give you a chance to work off the tension and anger you feel.

Pounding nails into a plank of wood is a good way to vent rage too. Writing a letter to your loved one (and crumpling it up), keeping a journal, or painting a picture of your feelings may also be useful outlets. Even watching a bruising football game on TV and cheering for your team can help to get the tension out.

On the other hand, you might also try meditation and relaxation tapes to help calm your nerves. Many people look to their religious beliefs to get them through hard times. Remember, it's okay to be angry with your circumstances and even with your loved one, but it is not acceptable to become abusive. If you need more help in dealing with your rage, seek out a trusted counselor, perhaps a member of the clergy, or a professional. Don't just let the feelings seethe inside you.

I feel isolated.   In his talk, Jerry Wise poignantly expressed his feelings of aloneness. No one understood. Extended-family members and friends didn't know how to deal with the situation. Even though Jerry and his family were surrounded by people who cared about and loved them, they still felt isolated.

Isolation often accompanies the caregiver's role. I will cover this issue more fully, along with suggestions on how to feel less alone, in Chapter 7.

I'm afraid my loved one will die (and sometimes—guiltily—I'm relieved by the thought).   Caregivers who endure months or years in constant fear of losing their family member often reach a point of feeling that they just can't take the stress anymore or can't bear to see the one they love continue to suffer.

Jimmy and I have watched his mother, his brother, Billy, and his sisters, Gloria and Ruth, all succumb to cancer within the span of a few years.

Jimmy's family's dying made us realize how fleeting life is. At any time, anything can change. We found ourselves making the most of the time left, being together with the family as much as possible.

When Jimmy's mother became ill, we visited her daily. We didn't discuss her condition, but reminisced about good times together and tried to honor her wish to remain at home with no help as long as possible. A great baseball fan, she watched whoever was playing every day on TV, and even went to bed at night with the radio turned on, listening to ball games on the

West Coast, never losing interest. And she took great pleasure in teasing us if "her team," the Dodgers, was ahead of the Atlanta Braves. She was a strong-willed and determined person who was able to retain some independence to the very end.

Ruth was an evangelist and had her religious faith to sustain her. Billy had his sense of humor. Billy underwent experimental therapies and suffered so much, though every time we saw him, he kept us laughing. He joked almost until the day he died. In fact, the day before he died, he asked to see the husband of the young nurse, Gail, who had been coming to his home regularly to give him shots to help ease the pain. When the husband arrived, Billy said, trying to appear serious, "Doug, before I die, I have to admit to you that Gail and I have been having an affair!" We felt uplifted from being with him.

We were out of the country when Gloria was diagnosed, and upon returning, we went straight to see her, even before going home. After witnessing the other family members suffer the same diagnosis, she knew what to expect. She accepted the fact that she was going to die and was content with it, at least when we were around. We used to visit her and wonder how she could be so calm and at ease.

Our sick family members clung to things that were really important to them and got as much pleasure from life as they could. In the end, with each one, we realized that they were at peace with themselves. It was those of us who would be left behind who were torn by the impending death.

COPING WITH YOUR LOVED ONE'S DEATH

Sadly, you may look ahead to the day when your loved one will die. Being a caregiver does not necessarily make the process any less difficult. There are practical and emotional issues to cope with.

Making arrangements for the funeral of the one you love is not easy. One has to think about the unthinkable. I know, because no sooner had we left the White House than I was approached by the director of ceremonies and special events of the Department of the Army about funeral arrangements for Jimmy. All former presidents must have contingency plans ready so that their funerals and associated events can be carried out on short notice, if necessary, and in an orderly fashion when the time comes. It was difficult for me, then, even knowing that Jimmy was well and healthy.

For the family of one who is chronically ill, there are many decisions that need to be made for the funeral—choosing the mortuary and cemetery plot, among other necessary details of the burial. Who will be called? Where will the wake be? It may be easier in the long run to make these arrangements earlier, while your loved one's death is not imminent, so family members won't have to go through these painful steps in a state of numbness, disbelief, and grief.

But there is also the emotional preparation for your ill family member's eventual death that must be considered. Sometimes death is seen as a blessing. If the one you are caring for agonizes beyond measure, it is not unmerciful to wish for an end to the suffering. But even if you have been grieving for years, the finality of death may come as a shock. Jerry Wise spoke of his son's passing:

It was a very sudden death. He went through Christmas and everything was fine. Late one afternoon, he started running a little fever and within six hours he died in my arms at home. So, even the death process itself—I wasn't prepared for it. Ten years of knowing, and still I wasn't prepared. He just died. But God was gracious and granted every wish we could have wished for in that death.

Perhaps that's the best that any of us can hope for at such a time.

As Jerry Wise struggled to put his life back together, he also talked compassionately about preparing for a loved one's passing:

The family of the terminally ill needs to understand and be involved. They need to understand the process of dying. They need to prepare themselves and prepare the terminally ill person for death. They should help children understand that the death is not a rejection—children often feel it as a deep rejection.

Grieving is a normal and natural part of life. People shouldn't be embarrassed by it. They need to express their feelings. They don't necessarily get over their loss, but they get through it. Dying is part of the normal process of life.

Just as you have prepared yourself for living with your loved one's chronic illness, so must you prepare yourself for the possibility of death.

Perhaps you can find some comfort in the lines of Dylan Thomas, one of my favorite poets:

> Do not go gentle into that good night.
> Rage, rage against the dying of the light.

Then, later, in another poem, Thomas expressed beautifully how our feelings can transcend tragedy:

> Though lovers be lost love shall not;
> And death shall have no dominion.

6.

CAREGIVING
AND FAMILY
HARMONY

Every family has conflicts—that's the nature of human relations. Most likely, some form of discord, even if minor, existed in your family before your loved one became ill. After all, it's not as if the lupus, brain tumor, or heart disease simply dropped in on a household that was completely devoid of problems.

Family disharmony doesn't suddenly disappear with the diagnosis of kidney failure or stroke either. Illness and the caregiving situation can worsen an already tense situation. Indeed, experts assert that caregiving often causes family friction and sometimes destroys the very relationship caregivers are trying so hard to preserve. In some instances, the illness can lead to family disruption, divorce, and alienation.

How does this happen? Guilt and anxiety can interfere with communication between you and your ill family member. You may have been experiencing all of the difficult emotions mentioned in Chapter 5, but are reluctant to express them for fear of further hurting your loved one. "She has enough to deal with," you may be thinking. "How can I bother her with my problems?" And so you keep silent, while your resentment builds to the boiling point.

For her part, the ill one may be envious of your good health or ashamed that she has brought this problem on the family. She is likely to feel defective or flawed and fear that no one in the family can ever understand her—after all, they're not sick—and so she, too, gives no voice to her concerns, and they fester within. With neither of you sharing your innermost thoughts, it's easy to see how intimacy and communication can break down.

You may also experience conflicts that are unique to your particular situation. If you are caring for a sick spouse, some issues will be different from those you will face if you're caring for an ailing parent or a child. Your family can pull together—or be pulled apart—in many different directions. Let's take a closer look at these particular dilemmas and how they can affect the dynamics within your family.

CARING FOR A SPOUSE

The long-term illness of a spouse can be devastating to one's marriage. In her touching book *Mainstay*, writer Maggie Strong candidly documents her personal and familial struggles as she cared for her husband, whose progressively deteriorating multiple sclerosis drove a wedge between them. Not only had she lost her husband's companionship, his wage-earning capacity, his sexual contact, his cooperation and partnership in the marriage, but she also believed that she had lost her present and her future. She felt herself being swallowed up by her husband's illness.

Strong calls the caregiving experience a "double whammy." "First you become a superman or superwoman," she writes. "Then you become invisible. Although you didn't notice when the situation was acute, you now see that the sick person is number one and you are number two." A shift in the balance of the relationship occurs. The caregiver is at once less important (since all the attention is focused on the ill spouse) and more important (since the full responsibility for the household, child-rearing, finances, and caregiving now lie squarely on the caregiver's shoulders alone).

Strong's experience was echoed in our CARE-NET surveys. Enid, whose husband suffers from kidney failure, described how totally dependent he became on her and how victimized she felt as a result:

> I give personal care such as shaving, bathing, administering medicine, and helping with exercise. He always has a physical or health problem. He will get over one and another will arise. He expects me to be there for him all the time, and it's very confining.
>
> My husband's illness has changed our relationship. I'm no longer the wife. I'm the mother. My husband acts like a child, constantly asking me for things, and he depends on me to make all the decisions. He cannot tolerate my frustration or my showing anger. He will become ill if I show anger and he will throw up. So I don't do anything to upset him. He ignores me if I try to talk about my feelings.

I feel constant pressure to take care of everything myself: the car, the house, the finances. I would like for my husband to be more appreciative of me and my role. He could help if he wants to, but he will fake not being able to care for himself to get my attention. He manipulates me.

Carla, whose husband suffers from a mental impairment, also experienced a shift in her marriage. Rather than feeling exploited, as Enid did, she believes that she is now the dominant member of the household.

I don't have a marriage as such. . . . I'm the benevolent manipulator, as my daughter calls me. My husband wanted to arrange our finances so I got him to consult a financial planner and made him think it was his idea. This relieved a lot of responsibility. . . . From the beginning of his illness until now, I have gone from an egalitarian to a dominant wife role. We have not had a physical relationship for four years.

Barbara Drucker, the president of the San Diego–based Well Spouse Foundation, explained in a *Los Angeles Times* article that if one must bathe and diaper one's spouse, or otherwise care for his or her intimate needs, sexuality can evaporate. "He or she becomes a patient, a child, not a spouse," she said. Mrs. Drucker and her ill husband have a mother-son relationship because he is so dependent. "That makes both of us angry," she added.

Dependency issues and the shift in the balance of power can be part of spousal caregiving. I know if something happened to me, I would feel like a burden on whoever had to take care of me all the time. I can't imagine the guilt I would feel if Jimmy had to do it. I would want to do everything I possibly could for myself. It would be hard for me to be waited on, even if I needed to be. But still, I speak in abstractions. I don't know how I would react when faced with the real situation. What courage it must take!

MAINTAINING YOUR MARRIAGE

Although Maggie Strong readily admits that some couples' difficulties are simply insoluble (for example, it may be impossible to rekindle sexual feelings or autonomy if a spouse is completely dependent physically or incapacitated), she does make some helpful suggestions based on the work of Dr. Florence Kaslow, a psychologist and family therapist who directs the Florida Couples and Family Institute in West Palm Beach. Some of these are:

1. *Allow the family unit more breathing room.* You may have to give up some of the exclusive relationship you have come to expect with your spouse. According to Dr. Kaslow, "If the couple clings to each other and one spouse says, 'I'll do it all,' they deplete themselves." Be open to others helping, including sitters, other family members, adult day-care centers, and nurses. You may need a break from caregiving, but your spouse may also need a break from you!

2. *Keep the lines of communication open.* If at all possible, share your feelings with your spouse. Although you may show a strong face to the world while agonizing inside, your loved one may interpret your silence as a lack of compassion or caring. This, of course, may be far from the truth.

Dr. Kaslow points out, however, that sometimes it's unwise

95

to disclose all of your feelings, since that might destroy your spouse's equilibrium. Still, she agrees, "it's good to have as much open communication as you can handle: otherwise the illness controls the couple." I'll have more information on how you can do this in the section on family meetings.

3. *Allow yourselves a full range of emotions.* You may find yourself becoming numbed by your experience. If you deny your fears, guilts, or anger and push them within, you may become depressed. You may also lose touch with your joyful emotions: how can you be happy when your loved one is suffering so, when you're feeling so burdened? Dr. Kaslow advises that you give vent to your full range of emotions. "It's important that the couple be sad and grieve and share pleasures." The ability to move from sadness to joy with each other is an element of a good marriage, in sickness and in health.

4. *Encourage independence.* If spouses are no longer able to earn a living, perhaps they can keep the family accounts in order and pay the bills. If they are wheelchair-bound and unable to do the marketing and cooking, perhaps they can plan the weekly menus and keep track of supplies in the pantry. It's vital to allow ill ones to use what capabilities they still possess. Otherwise, you turn them into children, and consequently, you may feel even more burdened. Sick partners need not be indulged or pampered, but should be encouraged to function at the highest possible level.

5. *Express empathy.* Sometimes, to understand others' behavior, you must see the world through their eyes. Expressing compassion and validating the emotions of those who are ill with statements such as "I really feel for you. You must be sad/angry/ upset about what's happening to your body" can go a long way in de-escalating potential conflicts. This gives sick ones permis-

sion to share their feelings, without your having to do anything.

6. *Seek counseling.* If you feel you and your spouse have reached an impasse, a competent counselor (psychiatrist, psychologist, clinical social worker, marriage counselor, or clergy) well versed in the issues families like yours face can help you sort through your emotions and concerns. You may find such an individual by asking for a referral from the physicians, nurses, or other professionals who deal with your partner's problem; other caregivers; or local, regional, or national illness-related associations (see Appendix B).

Family support groups can also be quite helpful. I'll have more on how to find one and what to look for in a good group in Chapter 7.

There is no shame in seeking assistance, especially if it helps you come to terms with your problems. If your spouse is unwilling or unable to attend the sessions, go on your own. Counseling can:

- provide you with emotional support and a shoulder to cry on, so you feel less alone.
- validate your experience.
- help you prioritize your many tasks, thereby relieving stress.
- encourage you to seek respite.
- furnish you with information about the illness and resources and referrals for equipment, care alternatives, etc.
- enhance the quality of your lives.
- enrich your remaining days together.

There is much to be gained by giving it a try. Indeed, counseling can be beneficial, whether you're providing care to a spouse, a parent, or a child.

CARING FOR A PARENT

While spouses may become overly dependent or withdraw from their usual responsibilities, elderly parents may try to maintain their independence at all costs—even when it is inappropriate. It is common for older people living at home to refuse to admit that they need care or to accept any alternatives.

Jimmy's mother, Miss Lillian, was a good example of this. Widowed in 1953, she lived alone for many years and was very independent. When Jimmy was president, she moved from her home in Plains to the "pond house," a few miles out of town. There were too many tourists in Plains knocking on her door! The pond house has always been a favorite family place. It is in the woods on the edge of a pond, and though small, with glass walls on two sides, it seems open and spacious. Miss Lillian loved it. She enjoyed the beauty of the pine trees and dogwood, fishing in the pond, and the privacy—with all the glass walls and windows, she never hung any curtains, even in the bedroom! She felt that secure and secluded.

Miss Lillian was still active, coming to the White House often to see us, representing both Jimmy and me at various functions. She stood in for me at a state dinner when I had to be away. She represented our country at the funeral of the president of India, which was a homecoming for her. She had been in the Peace Corps in India many years earlier.

Then, in 1980, she fell and broke her hip. After the accident, she couldn't get out or around much. In fact, for a long time, she couldn't get out at all. She used a walker and eventually a cane but soon fell again and hurt herself once more. This time she entered a nursing home in Americus for several weeks of physical therapy.

When she came home, the family strongly believed Miss Lillian needed someone to take care of her, so she hired a nurse, Rachel, who was supposed to stay day and night. That didn't last very long! Miss Lillian didn't like another person in the house with her all the time. So Rachel began to stay only in the daytime, but that wasn't good either. Miss Lillian insisted she got along better alone in her home. However, she did want Jimmy to come and check on her every day.

This was soon after we had come home from the White House, and Jimmy and I had not yet gotten very deeply involved in outside activities. We were writing our autobiographies and planning the Carter Center, so we were at home in Plains most of the time. We went to see Miss Lillian every day when we could, and had good visits. Usually some other family members would be there, particularly one granddaughter with her baby, which was a joy for Miss Lillian.

But the situation was far from ideal. Miss Lillian still had trouble walking and had to sit most of the time. An avid reader, though, she read and watched television and dealt with an impressive amount of correspondence that she received from admirers all over the country. She tried to stay busy, but we all worried about her being alone and felt responsible for her. We didn't know how to help her in ways that we felt were appropriate, mostly because she wouldn't let us. We did equip her bathroom with railings and a special shower chair and we took her some of her meals. Still, it was hard for her to admit that she needed our help.

Another family problem that often arises when caring for an ailing parent is the caregiver's resentment of siblings. It seems that in each family, usually one child (most often a daughter) becomes the responsible one. Unfortunately, often her siblings don't help adequately. Research shows that relatives other than the primary caregiver rarely provide significant levels of care. This can happen for a variety of reasons:

- The parent wants only one child to care for him or her and refuses attention from anyone else.
- The caregiver isn't assertive enough in demanding help from other members of the family.
- The siblings are in denial. They may refuse to cooperate or may ignore the situation altogether.
- The caregiver is unwilling to let go of the reins and share the task, even when exhausted by it.
- The siblings live far away, and it is difficult for them to help.
- Siblings who work outside the home may feel that a sibling homemaker is the only one with enough free time to assume the caregiving burden.
- Siblings who contribute financially may feel they have given enough support.
- Male siblings may hold the old-fashioned belief that caregiving is exclusively a woman's job.

At times it may be the ill parent who foments the family power struggles. A speaker at one of the Rosalynn Carter Institute meetings talked to us about the resentment she feels toward her sister:

Jean lived with her mother, who suffered from heart disease, and cared for her full-time. She said she encouraged her mother's independence as part of her treatment. The younger daughter, Gladys, came by only occasionally, but when she did come, Jean said, "She pampers Mother, doing for her what I

Caregiving and Family Harmony

think she can do on her own. And when she leaves, my mother always says to me, 'Now there goes my *good* daughter!' "

Apparently Jean is not alone in her frustration. Dr. Gregory C. Smith and a team of psychologists at the Ringel Institute of Gerontology at the State University of New York, Albany, examined the problems identified during the counseling of fifty-one daughters and daughters-in-law who cared for elderly parents. Most of the caregivers in this study felt angry, abandoned, unappreciated, and abused by their siblings. "Although these women had assumed primary responsibility for the care of their parent without coercion," the researchers noted, "they were resentful when siblings neither appreciated their diligence as caregivers nor offered to provide help."

Eloise Paschal, one of the speakers at the Fourth Annual Conference of the Rosalynn Carter Institute, voiced similar concerns as she described her caregiving duties in relation to the rest of her family. One of a family of two sisters and three brothers, Eloise had been designated "the boss."

When Mama decided to take the surgery for cancer and went into the hospital, "the boss" was the one chosen by the other siblings to make the decisions: What's going to happen to Mama when she leaves the hospital? Who's going to be there?

I was that person. For thirteen years, I rode the highway from Americus, Georgia, to South Carolina once a month. The last two years of Mama's life, I went every weekend. I tried to bring her to Georgia but she didn't want to give up her church or her Wednesday senior citizen outings. The boys in the family didn't want her left alone at all. All of us were long distance. One brother lived fifty miles away from her, so he tried to have contact with her every day. But when he had to be out of town, he would call me to come over. . . .

When it really got down to the final time, and the hospice people came out to talk to her, we had a lot of social service support. But we needed Mama to accept that she needed help. At every service the social worker would offer her, she would say, "I don't need this, I have five children." Well, each one of us had our own families and lived away from her. We had to work in order to live. . . .

And then I got to the place of being the family caregiver. Mama went to the hospital one last time and the doctor told us she couldn't go home unless she had twenty-four-hour care. Well, "the boss" was the person she wanted. She didn't trust my sister to cook or give her medicine on time. I was the one with the caring, supportive husband, so I left Americus and went to South Carolina to stay with Mama until her death.

As Mrs. Paschal delivered her talk quickly and matter-of-factly, I wondered where her brothers were in all of this. Why hadn't they or their wives taken a more active role? How could they make so many demands and yet not pitch in? Why hadn't Eloise been more insistent in requiring their involvement? She said that in order to keep peace in the family she hadn't protested. But at what cost to herself? It's easy to see how a caregiver in Eloise Paschal's position could resent her siblings.

FAMILY MEETINGS HELP BRIDGE THE GAP

Eloise might have had an easier time of it if she and her family had held family meetings to air their feelings and brainstorm other caregiving options before she was saddled with the full responsibility.

Family meetings can be a practical way to solve some of the problems that arise when a parent needs care. These gatherings need not be used exclusively to solve problems with the care of ailing parents. They are also beneficial if the difficulty involves an ill spouse or child. They may, however, be difficult to arrange for some families, particularly for those whose members are in denial or don't want to assume any responsibility. Family meetings are a good idea, though, even when things are running smoothly, to keep all members posted on the condition of the ill parent. And if you're having problems, as most families do, they can be especially valuable.

You can hold these meetings regularly, say, once a month or by appointment. Sometimes unexpected emergencies make them necessary. Be sure to set the agenda before beginning. You might want to discuss how to deal with Dad's independent streak, your siblings' involvement, or your own need for respite. If you try to cover too much ground in one meeting, the issues may become muddled.

If you feel you can't run the meeting by yourself because you are too exhausted or upset, invite a trusted and experienced counselor, pastor, gerontologist, or social worker to facilitate the communication and provide suggestions for resources and solutions.

Don't confuse the discussion by bringing in extraneous complaints and ancient history. This may be difficult if you have pent-up feelings because of a lack of support from the family, but it is necessary if the meeting is going to be successful. Focus on the positive actions family members can take from this meeting.

See to it that phone calls or other distractions do not disrupt your session. Family members who are unable to attend because they live far away might maintain contact with the group by phone. Conference calls with speakerphones can also be arranged so that everyone is involved. A family member might wish to take notes and mail them to the participants so that all agree on what has been accomplished. It would be wise to send a copy of the meeting's "minutes" to absentee family members as well.

During these meetings, each person must get equal time to have his or her say. Each must feel heard. If ill parents are capable of participating, by all means they should be included; they would not like having their fate decided without some input. Equality in the discussion helps all of your family members feel important and engenders a sense of responsibility and the sense that "we're all in this together."

Be careful how you explain your state of mind. Inappropriately expressed feelings, including accusations and "guilt trips," can cause big arguments. Instead of approaching the issues with "Why don't you ever . . ." or "You never do anything . . . ," you can begin by saying, "I know that with your working hours it will be hard for you to . . ." or "I know that having to pitch in the fifty dollars a month that Mother needs for —— will be a sacrifice for you." This will let the others know that you understand their position, and they are more likely to cooperate.

But be sure your family knows how you feel. Don't pull any punches or hide the true meaning of your words. Avoid saying, "I hate to bother you because you're all so busy," when you really mean, "I can't go on like this. I need help." Try to specify the types of help you need and elicit from family members exactly how they will respond.

After all, you are a family. If you communicate appropriately, the chances are that the family can be brought closer together despite the difficulties you share.

CARING FOR A DISABLED CHILD

The birth of a child is a joyous but stressful event in the life of any family. Routines must be readjusted. The baby can seem insatiable in its demands for care. When the child is disabled or ill, the stress is multiplied many times over. Parents fear for their youngster's survival. They worry about developmental delays and social adjustment. They experience additional financial strains. They may even feel guilt and shame if they have given birth to a less-than-perfect child. They brood that perhaps they were at fault in some way.

The situation becomes a vicious cycle. The more severe the disability, the greater the level of stress, and the more difficult the family adjustment.

Parents of disabled children often worry about their youngsters' care if they should no longer be able to provide it. In our CARE-NET study, the father of a child with cerebral palsy expressed this common fear when asked what would happen to his daughter if he were out of the picture. "Jennifer's needs probably wouldn't get met as well as if we were taking care of her," he fretted. "I would be very unhappy and worried for a long time about whether others were doing as good a job as we would."

It is common for a child born with disabilities or one who becomes disabled due to an accident or illness to be one of several siblings in an otherwise healthy family. In his talk at the Rosalynn Carter Institute Conference (see Chapter 5), Jerry Wise mentioned how important it was for him to keep his other two children's lives as normal as possible while he cared for his youngest son. Families that care for a disabled child often fear that the illness or the child's presence may be damaging to the other children in the home.

It is true that a disabled child may increase family discord. Siblings are often jealous of the extra attention their brother or sister is receiving, and if they're older they may remember what life was like before the problems began. They may feel angry that their sister's misbehavior will go unpunished, while they must pay the consequences. They may feel awkward at having to explain their brother's appearance or behavior to classmates or friends. And they may sometimes take it out on the disabled one by teasing or nagging because he or she is "different." Or they can feel frustrated or guilty that they can't (or shouldn't) pick a fight with their sibling, as other kids do.

Some well siblings take on caregiving responsibilities such as babysitting either because they're asked to or because they feel it is their duty. They may even feel the need to "overachieve" to make up for what they perceive as their parents' disappointment over the disabled child. Not surprisingly, they may feel resentful of these extra pressures and obligations.

And parents, feeling sorry for their ill child's disability, may find themselves overindulging and coddling that sibling at the expense of the other youngsters in the household.

In some cases, the able-bodied children may receive preferential treatment. This occurred in one of our CARE-NET families. During the survey, a mother angrily described how her brother had offered to take only her well children for a summer visit, excluding her mentally retarded daughter, who surely would have missed her siblings. "She, also, would have felt slighted if I had let the others go," the mother said.

On the other hand, it is the parents, too, who may favor the well children in the family. This can happen because of feelings of guilt, when parents realize that so much of their attention has to go to the disabled one. But sometimes, out of frustration and resentment of the disability, parents have been known to abuse the disabled one.

Clearly, children are not the only ones who can be insensitive and self-centered!

HELPING YOUR FAMILY ADJUST

Although parents often fear that having a child with a disability in the home may be damaging to their other children, recent research has shown that this is not necessarily true.

In a *New York Times* article on disabled children, the psychologist Dr. Stanley D. Klein, editor-in-chief of *Exceptional Parent* magazine, explained that a disabled child can add stress to the household, but his or her presence is not necessarily damaging. "It can lead to creative problem-solving and personal growth," Dr. Klein stated. Siblings gain "a greater appreciation of the value of different kinds of people and are more understanding of human differences."

The article provided several suggestions that I'm sure you'll find useful in helping your children make the adjustment:

1. *Provide appropriate information.* Even though they live with it daily, the other youngsters in the family will need to understand your disabled child's condition. Explain why this sibling looks and acts differently. Tailor the discussion to your child's level of understanding. A four-year-old may understand that Jason has a problem in his brain without your having to explain about neurons and dendrites!

2. *Give reassurance.* Young children often believe that they are to blame for negative occurrences. It is therefore important for you to reassure them that they had nothing to do with their sibling's condition. They also may be frightened that the ailment is contagious. Again, your reassurance will help relieve their anxieties. Adolescents may need your promise that although you will tend to your ill child's needs for as long as you can, they will be free to attend college and have a life of their own.

3. *Help them with social skills.* Your youngsters may have to face their playmates' or classmates' curiosity about their sibling's condition. Help them practice answers to their friends' potentially embarrassing questions so that they feel at ease in responding.

4. *Arrange for special time.* Each child deserves your undivided attention, if only for short periods each day. Take the time to be with your well children, to find out about their day, their problems and concerns. This will help reduce jealousy.

5. *Validate your children's feelings.* Like adults, your well children may have many emotions regarding the situation in the house-

hold. They may feel that it is unfair that their sibling is receiving the lion's share of your time and resources. Allow them to vent their feelings and let them know that it's normal for them to feel jealous or angry. Dr. Klein advises you to "let your children know that it's okay to have negative feelings toward the disabled sibling. They're not bad kids, and you won't reject them because they have these feelings." You might find the suggestions for family meetings useful in this regard.

6. *Seek out a sibling support group.* These groups have sprung up only recently. In them, well siblings share social activities and sometimes emotions they find too difficult to reveal to their parents. Your local social service agency or illness association may know of some groups in your area (see Appendix B for some resources).

To the best of your ability, try to treat your children equally. If possible, all family rules should be observed by all children. Consistency helps your children—healthy or ill—feel safe and cared for.

Family dilemmas may seem insoluble but often they can be resolved if you and your family members maintain a feeling of goodwill and a sense of common purpose. However, if you have no one close to rely on or if you cannot get the support you need from your relatives, you might find it helpful to turn to a family of peers: other caregivers who struggle with issues similar to yours. That is the subject of the next chapter.

7.

DEALING WITH YOUR ISOLATION

I had no one I could call and talk to. I had no one for support. I had no one for advice. We were in a new area. I had no friends, and I stood alone.

I sympathized with my husband's condition. I love my husband. We were married twenty years at the time; we're going on twenty-six now. I'm going to stand with him, whatever happens. . . . But we caregivers are going through things, and we feel like we're the invisible people. We're the ones who are shouldering the family, we're shouldering the finances, we're responsible for these individuals emotionally, mentally, and physically. Where's our support? We're not professionals. We haven't taken one single course in this field and yet we're supposed to handle these crises all alone.

These were Sandra Wolfenbarger's tearful words as she addressed the Fifth Annual Conference of the Rosalynn Carter

Institute on October 28, 1993. Fortunately, Sandra has found support for herself as she continues to care for her severely depressed husband. She is currently the chairperson of the regional chapter of the Alliance for the Mentally Ill. And she's on the board of directors of the local Mental Health Association.

But how many other caregivers across the nation suffer from the same feelings of aloneness, alienation, and desperation? As a result of my involvement in this field, I have found that, unfortunately, many do. The stigma of illness often rubs off on the caregivers. No one is interested in their plight. Like Sandra, many caregivers feel that no one cares. Friends may drop in from time to time, but as I have mentioned earlier, caregivers sense that they're doing so as a duty, out of pity. Or if others do care, they are sometimes at a loss to know how to behave or respond. Feeling helpless and awkward, they may shy away from the situation.

Researchers point out that when caregivers perceive themselves as being alone and in "second place" with no one to talk to or help out, they often feel trapped—literally imprisoned in their own households. These feelings can lead to intense anger and depression, which can further drive away friends and family.

The isolation may be physical. Some caregivers are unable to leave their homes because of their loved one's constant needs. Nancy, for example, sold the family car and truck after her husband became immobilized due to Parkinson's disease. "My husband is totally dependent on me," she acknowledged during her CARE-NET interview. "I have help bathing him during the week, but on weekends, I do it all: bathing, shaving, hair, changing linens, preparing meals, feeding, cleaning. I turn him all during the night and get up and change him.

"I don't do anything but stay home," she continued. "I even get my haircuts and perms here. My children do all my shopping. There's nobody around here—no support groups. Friends come, but they can't know what it's like until they go through this."

Other caregivers feel both physically and emotionally isolated. Another respondent interviewed in our CARE-NET study explained how friends and relatives have avoided him ever since his son was diagnosed with schizophrenia. "The stigma of a mental disorder causes you to lose many friends," Tom said with some bitterness. "Even family members back off; they're not around very much. I feel shunned by them. Our friends and family have not been supportive."

And Catherine complained angrily about her aloneness during her interview. Even though she had already placed her father in a nursing home after a series of devastating strokes, she, too, felt emotionally isolated.

"No other family members visit or care for Dad the way I do," she explained. "My son visits him once a month. Other relatives visit seldom with no care provided. My brother sends flowers on Father's Day. I have no moral or physical support. I desire someone to go with me to the nursing home but no one volunteers, and I don't want to ask. I feel so cut off—no one gives a damn. I'm the only one who cares."

Perhaps the worst feeling of all is that of being the sole individual in the world to whom these frightful things are happening.

THE NEED FOR PEER SUPPORT

When we asked the informal caregivers in our CARE-NET study to rate what they felt were their most pressing concrete needs and those that were the least adequately addressed in their communities, a prominent item on their list—second only to community resources such as hospitals, day-care centers, and services for the homebound—was "linkage with other caregivers."

We found that caregivers need to spend time with other caregivers. They derive much from sharing with others in the same situation. It's the best way to fight isolation—to reverse the feeling that you are the only one in the world with these problems. We recognized this when we saw how much healing took place as a result of caregivers telling their stories to others who understood them during the CARE-NET interviews. Sharing with other caregivers continues to be an important element of our Rosalynn Carter Institute program.

One of my correspondents, Rosemarie Mitchell, who is caring for her severely disabled son, even believes that the state should employ family caregivers to advise their peers about practical matters. In a speech to the Governor's Council on Developmental Disabilities in Americus, Georgia, on July 17, 1992, she declared:

> Caregivers need advice, not orders, about equipment that would aid in the care of their family member. A great deal of this advice and support can be provided by someone such as myself and others who have experienced and found answers and sources for many of our own similar problems. In England, they encourage and even hire persons with handicaps

to counsel and give moral support to those who need it. This provides employment for the handicapped individuals. Plus it helps others to perhaps find a way to help cope with their disabilities, sources needed in providing a productive daily lifestyle, and the ability to help others. In other words, Stop paying the Ph.D.'s for their word-of-mouth information! Get the information from those who know and care.

Peer support groups can be an important source of such first-hand information. They may also be crucial for your own well-being. They can:

- help you learn more about your loved one's condition, including treatments, prognosis, and what the future may hold.
- provide information about the best community resources (including day-care centers and home-care nursing), the most responsive professionals, and the latest equipment that may help the one you are caring for become more mobile as it relieves some of your burden.
- create networking connections so that you will have access to the best care possible.
- lessen the sense of stigma associated with the disabled one's illness.
- give you an opportunity to joke and laugh about your circumstances with people who really understand and won't judge you.
- give you an opportunity to cry and complain without others urging you to "buck up" or making you feel guilty about your own needs and pain.
- give you a moment to focus on just you.
- alleviate your aloneness by introducing you to new friends who *do* understand.

- help you brainstorm solutions to your problems.
- relieve stress and help you feel more in control of your life.
- give you hope as you listen to how others have coped in similar situations.

In her book *Mainstay*, Maggie Strong wrote about her first encounter with a support group for spouses of people with multiple sclerosis. The informal group consisted of five women, two who were older than Maggie and two who were younger.

> We "younger" three had been strangers lost in Asia. Crossing the steppes, we'd stumbled upon two English-speaking travelers and had been relieved to hear that they knew the same nouns as we did, the same verbs. We spoke the same language and didn't have to apologize for or explain our pronunciation. We could ask Marianne and Eleanor for directions.

Clearly the peer support group was helpful for Maggie, as it is for hundreds of thousands of other caregivers across the nation who have otherwise felt "lost in Asia"! Maybe it will also be helpful for you.

THE MAKINGS OF AN EFFECTIVE GROUP

Caregiver support groups come in all shapes and sizes. Many meet once a week or once a month. Some are time-limited, with a predetermined number of members, while others are more open-ended: they meet continuously and invite new members to join. Some focus on a particular illness; some are established for all caregivers or exclusively for spouses or children of ailing individuals. Some are rather formalized, with leaders and invited expert speakers who share information on the latest medications, equipment, and research developments. Some spring up spontaneously—a group of neighbors get together to talk about their common problems. Some meet in hospitals, as a part of the social work department's continuing care. Some are offshoots of national organizations. Some even put out their own newsletters with tips on how to cope and profiles of members and their trials and triumphs.

According to Suzanne G. Mintz, family caregiver and cofounder of the National Family Caregivers Association, based in Silver Spring, Maryland, effective groups don't just happen. They take some work. Indeed, the structure of a group—whether it's focused on one illness or on caregivers in general—is less important than whether it's actually capable of buoying its members' spirits. The editors of the National Family Caregivers Association newsletter, *Take Care!*, have compiled the factors they believe enhance a group's effectiveness. I would like to share these with you here.

A support group is effective when it has:

- a caring atmosphere and a sense of trust between group members.
- a comfortable mix among the participants that creates and builds bonds.
- a structure and purpose that gives the group focus.
- an agreement on group rules.

Also, the group should have a problem-solving, pragmatic approach to situations, focusing on available options and choices as a way of increasing feelings of control.

Often these goals are reached with the hard work of a group

leader or facilitator. Leaders can be therapists such as marriage and family counselors, clinical social workers, or psychologists, or they can be others who are able to create structure and a feeling of safety within the group. According to the National Association of Family Caregivers, effective group leaders:

- are good listeners.
- are empathetic yet able to react to the situations discussed with some objectivity.
- are able to build trust and draw others out.
- can recognize when a group member needs special attention and can make referrals to professionals.
- know how to keep the group's attention on shared concerns as it moves forward.
- maintain group guidelines and rules and prevent one member from hurting another or the group as a whole.
- make each member feel special and provide everyone with the opportunity to participate. (Remember, sometimes simply listening can be a highly beneficial form of participation.)
- can control the flow of information so that no group member feels overwhelmed.

Leaderless groups such as the one in which Maggie Strong participated can also be effective if the members show caring and respect for one another's struggles.

HOW TO FIND A SUPPORT GROUP

If you live in a large or mid-size city, you may find many support groups already in place. Contact the following resources to locate a group in your area:

- your family member's nurse, doctor, or social worker
- hospitals and nursing homes in your area
- local chapters of national health organizations such as the National Multiple Sclerosis Society, the American Diabetes Association, the American Lung Association, or other health or self-help information clearinghouses (see Appendix B)
- your county health department
- your local council on aging
- the state department of social services
- nonprofit social service agencies such as Catholic Charities or the Jewish Family Service
- private clinical social workers specializing in chronic illnesses or gerontology
- clergy (some congregations may even sponsor their own groups)
- government information hotlines

CREATING YOUR OWN SUPPORT GROUP

What if you're living in a town that does not have a caregivers' peer support group? It may not be easy, but you can start your own.

That's exactly what Sara "Sissy" Bowen did in Americus. Sissy is a thirty-two-year-old college graduate who moved back home in 1989 to take care of her grandmother "GaSara," who was experiencing the middle to late stage of Alzheimer's disease. In a long letter to me Sissy chronicled how she fought isolation:

Over the four years that I have been here caring for GaSara, I have watched this disease slowly destroy the woman who raised me. About a year and a half ago, due to the insight of my dearest friend, I began to realize that the disease was destroying me, as well. I began to look for help.

I called the local Council on Aging, the hospital, the nursing homes, all of the obvious places . . . and was dismayed to find no help available . . . not even a brochure about Alzheimer's! My friend saw the Alzheimer's Association's toll-free number on the television. She called the number and the information they sent us opened a flood gate of insight and inspiration.

We learned a lot immediately. We found out that 4 million Americans probably have Alzheimer's, and most of them are cared for by family, at home. We learned we are far from being alone. We also discovered that there are seven Alzheimer's Association chapters in Georgia. When I began calling these chapters, I was encouraged by hearing the invaluable services that they offer. However, I was saddened as I realized that our area had not yet been included in a chapter.

Only weeks after making this discovery, I read an article in the *Times Recorder,* submitted by Mickey Holloway . . . asking for response from anyone interested in forming an Alzheimer's support group. I contacted Mickey immediately and we met soon after that. About six weeks later, our group was formed. Mickey had rolled the ball to me . . . I took it . . . and have been rolling with it ever since!

The Middle Flint Area Alzheimer's Support Group has been meeting since 1992. The group has sixty-four members ranging in age from nineteen to ninety-one, including spouses, siblings, children, grandchildren, and in-laws, and a growing mailing list of more than eight hundred families and professionals. With state funding, the group was able to establish a much needed Alzheimer's respite program and is involved in creating a dementia-specific adult day-care center. And recently the Middle Flint area was chosen as a model site to benefit from a $320,000 Alzheimer's demonstration grant to initiate mobile day care; a care management, assessment, and referral program; and community education and training. Sissy has been hired to coordinate development of the grant.

Sissy Bowen and Mickey Holloway connected with a national organization to form their group, but support can come from many sources. In Plains, several women whose husbands had died got together to form a Pals' Club. Today, twenty-five widows are involved. Each is assigned a pal within the group. They meet once a month, and since many are elderly and live alone in big houses, the pals phone one another daily to be sure they are all right.

Certainly you could set up a Pals' Club if you know two or three other caregivers in your community. A kindhearted phone call from someone who really understands can do so much to brighten your day. Besides, this sort of network would demand very little effort or money. It wouldn't even require that you leave your home—an important consideration if you have difficulty locating a sitter or other respite care.

If you are more ambitious and have more energy, you can create a group like Sissy and Mickey's. It is not impossible. As Dr. Leonard Felder explains in his book *When a Loved One Is Ill,* "Most of the thousands of support groups that exist today were started not too long ago by someone like yourself who said, 'There's got to be other people who are working on similar issues. . . .' "

To get your own support group started:

1. *Contact physicians, nurses, social workers, hospitals, nursing homes, and other professionals and institutions in your area that have worked with others suffering from the same ailment as your loved one.* Ask them to publicize your meetings to patients, family members, colleagues, and organizations.

2. *Call the national self-help clearinghouses (listed in Appendix B) and ask for advice, contacts, and printed guidelines on starting a support group.*

3. *Ask national clearinghouses for similar organizations in your state.* Let national and local clearinghouses know of your new support group so they can refer others to your meetings.

4. *Some group members prefer personal sharing during meetings whereas others (usually those relatively new to the caregiving role) need practical information and resources.* Be sure to allow for both types of support at each meeting.

To find potential members, post fliers in doctors' offices and on nursing-home and hospital bulletin boards—anywhere that caregivers may congregate. If you are really energetic, you can submit an article or press release to your local newspaper and TV and radio stations. Ask the media to promote your group as a public service or to do a feature story about your program.

Most local media are looking for good human interest stories in their communities. If you affiliate with a national health association, as Sissy Bowen did, you might receive organizational help and advice from the parent group.

TURNING TO YOUR RELIGIOUS INSTITUTION

As part of our CARE-NET study, we asked whether the family caregivers in our area looked to their religious institutions to alleviate some of their isolation and their burden. This is, after all, southwest Georgia, the heart of the "Bible Belt," and we anticipated that many would find solace in their church.

Some of the responses we received were startling at the very least. As expected, 86 percent of the informal caregivers said that their religious beliefs were very important to their lives. Seventy percent said that their church provided them spiritual guidance that helped them with their caregiving. During the interviews, family caregivers often disclosed that they turned to prayer and belief in God as their source of strength.

But when we asked family caregivers how much concrete support (such as money, respite, transportation, or supplies) they received from their religious institutions, only 10 percent replied that they received help! And more than two-thirds of our participants said that their church was providing inadequate assistance.

I suppose I shouldn't have been so surprised by this. When I was teaching Sunday school before Jimmy became governor, every year my class would put together a basket of food and canned goods for a needy family. But we didn't know who to give it to. We had to go to the Welfare Department to find an impoverished family. The church couldn't tell us which families in our community needed help.

Why aren't religious institutions more involved in providing direct, hands-on assistance to families who are struggling to maintain their equilibrium under difficult circumstances? Virginia Schiaffino, executive director of the National Federation of Interfaith Volunteer Caregivers, Inc., in Kingston, New York, explained the problems during her address to the Fourth Annual Conference of the Rosalynn Carter Institute on October 22, 1992.

"In times of trouble in this country, the first place people turn is their congregation," Ms. Schiaffino said. "As people of faith, they go back and expect their congregation to be supportive of them. But often congregations don't respond because the clergy have multiple responsibilities, and in many instances, are overwhelmed by the number of demands placed on their time by the religious sector and their congregations." She also noted that often the minister has a full-time job elsewhere. Indeed, some congregations have only part-time or traveling clergy because there are too few to staff all of the congregations around the country.

In addition, many religious organizations simply lack the funds to hire a social worker who could administer or carry out such a helping program. Moreover, often volunteers are not trained appropriately to respond to the request for help.

Still, I believe that churches, synagogues, mosques, and temples should be more active in their communities; they should know about the needs of their congregants—especially caregivers—and help eliminate their sense of isolation. When a member falls ill, we all pray for him or her and the minister goes to

123

the hospital or home to visit, but I think religious institutions should take a more active role in informing people about health issues and in helping with some of the caregivers' practical problems, including transportation and respite.

One of the programs at the Carter Center in Atlanta is an Interfaith Health Program, designed to help individual churches and faith communities provide information about basic health care to their congregations. Since so many health problems are caused by our own personal habits—smoking, drinking alcohol, improper diet, lack of exercise—we began this program to inform people about these issues. The purpose in designing the program, though, was twofold: to help congregations better serve their own members, but also to help them reach out to those whom the current health-care system does not encompass because of their poverty, joblessness, homelessness, or for other reasons.

More than 70 percent of churches, synagogues, mosques, and temples in our country have at least one health program that serves those living in their communities. At a conference recently at the Carter Center, we assembled Christians, Muslims, Jews, Hindus, Buddhists, and others, all of whom were working in health care through community-based efforts of their congregations. We explored ideas and discussed ways that we could develop a resource center for helping faith groups become more active in the health field. We believe that even if this nation finally achieves universal health-care coverage, there will still be a need for the faith community to be involved.

Working in the poverty area of Atlanta, we have learned that even when health care is available, people don't always take advantage of it, because they don't know it is available, they don't have transportation, they are intimidated by doctors, or they are resigned to a life of hopelessness. As Jimmy has often said, congregations could make sure that every pregnant woman in their immediate neighborhood gets prenatal care, that every child is immunized by age two, and that every housebound elderly person gets a check-in telephone call daily.

The various religions have traditionally, as part of their ministry, established hospitals and clinics to assist those who need help. In today's environment, this is too expensive. What better way is there for individual members of congregations to put their faith into action than by helping others in need?

This kind of program provides a great opportunity for the faith community to help caregivers. Indeed, this is already being done in many communities across our country.

INTERFAITH VOLUNTEER CAREGIVERS —A GODSEND

The National Federation of Interfaith Volunteer Caregivers has provided a solution to this pressing dilemma. This not-for-profit organization was established in 1984 by the Robert Wood Johnson Foundation, the largest health-care foundation in the United States, to promote the ministry of caregiving.

Today, the National Federation of Interfaith Volunteer Caregivers works with more than three hundred coalitions of congregations throughout forty-five states, the District of Columbia, the Territory of Guam, and Canada. On the average, each coalition mobilizes about seven hundred volunteers from thirty diverse congregations within a community. Each serves about seven hundred individuals and families. Volunteer caregivers give two to four hours per week.

And the program continues to grow. In July 1993, the Robert

Wood Johnson Foundation established the Faith in Action Program, which will fund an additional 920 Interfaith Volunteer Caregiver projects and will make available eighteen-month start-up grants of $25,000 for each new group.

Who are interfaith volunteer caregivers? Simply people of all ages—the youngest is about five, the oldest is a hundred and one—who wish to put their faith into action through volunteer work. Seventy-six percent are recruited directly from congregations and see this activity as their ministry. They often tell the directors of the programs that what they do is between themselves and their God. They want neither recognition nor reimbursement. It is the first time that many have volunteered for anything.

Interfaith volunteer caregivers help everyone regardless of age, race, or religion, and they do so without any attempt to proselytize. They do not replace formal service providers in the community but, rather, fill in the gaps. Motivated by faith, the volunteers quickly develop a lasting relationship with the people they serve and often become family to one another. They receive training by professionals so that they are comfortable, confident, and competent when called upon to provide assistance.

The volunteers offer a broad range of services. Rose Nakamura is the administrator of one of the interfaith volunteer caregivers' programs in Hawaii. This program, begun in 1990, is called Project Dana and is based on the Buddhist principle of *dana*, which in Sanskrit means "selfless giving" of time and energy. Mrs. Nakamura and Shim Kanazawa, the founder, now have four hundred volunteers who are serving six hundred persons and who by 1993 had rendered a total of more than

35,000 hours of service. In this particular program, volunteers assist the frail elderly. They provide:

- friendly home and telephone visits
- respite and relief for primary caregivers (see Chapter 8)
- transportation to medical appointments, grocery shopping, and religious services
- minor home repairs and maintenance
- light housekeeping
- hospital, nursing-home, and home-care visits

In 1993, Rose Nakamura was the recipient of the first Rosalynn Carter Caregiving Award.

Some of the program volunteers commented on their efforts:

Ethel, who helps an eighty-nine-year-old caregiver of a homebound sister, said, "Providing transportation was my initial assignment, but this is really secondary. My 'participant' looks forward to being picked up every week, going out, and talking to someone who listens to her problems. This is a time of respite for her."

And Jessie finds Project Dana "a commendable program, that renders tremendous service . . . and goes toward the making of a better community and society for all." She has been helping an eighty-three-year-old, living with a partially paralyzed husband, do her marketing and shopping. "At first my participant seemed to have the impression that my service may not last for long. She was buying a lot of unperishables to stock up her larder. I reassured her that as long as I have to do my own shopping, I will take her along. . . . Going shopping is such an enjoyable outing for her. I feel rewarded just by seeing how happy this makes her." Jessie and her participant have been going shopping for three years now!

According to Virginia Schiaffino, the growing national movement is built on the following three premises:

1. *Every faith has a basic calling to reach out to those who hurt.* Theological differences are of little importance; all people share the common call to put their faith into action and help those who need it. The National Federation of Interfaith Volunteer Caregivers has worked with Buddhists, Mennonites, Muslims, and people from the Native American traditions, as well as with adherents of mainline Judaism and Christianity.

2. *Resources are scarce.* When individuals and families looking for support find that there are long waiting lists for services or that they are ineligible to receive some of those services and therefore are without financial means to purchase them, they are left feeling despair, abandonment, and anxiety. They don't know where to turn. Faith communities can be there for them.

3. *Helping creates a sense of community.* If congregations could come together, put their theological differences aside, and establish a coalition dedicated to the ministry of caregiving, then they could create an effective program that responds to needs both within the congregation and in the wider community. The program would be enduring because it generates community support.

To illustrate how interfaith volunteer caregivers can help you, the family caregiver, Ms. Schiaffino told me about Will, a postman in Washington D.C. Will's wife, Alicia, had attempted suicide. When she was discharged from the hospital a week before Christmas, Will was told that he could not leave her alone; the holidays are particularly dangerous for people suffering from severe depression.

But Will was unable to take off from work during the busiest mail season of the year. He appealed to his local Interfaith

Volunteer Caregiver project for help. The project director responded by organizing teams of trained volunteers to sit with Alicia day and night.

Will could not believe that strangers would give up their Christmas to help him. After all, spending time with someone who is suicidal can be frightening. Besides, the volunteers were sacrificing hours they would otherwise devote to cooking and shopping and being with their families. Their acts of kindness strengthened Will, relieved him, and eventually brought him back to the church. They even bolstered Alicia's resolve.

I imagine that Sandra Wolfenbarger, Nancy, Tom, and Catherine, the caregivers whom we met at the beginning of this chapter, would have felt less isolated and desperate had they made contact with interfaith caregiving groups. Perhaps you will too. If you do not know of a group near you, see Appendix B for the address and phone number of the National Federation headquarters.

Just as we all have our own style of caregiving, we seek out help from others based on our personal needs. Only you can decide what kind of support suits you best. But please do seek it out. No one should have to go through the experience of caregiving alone. You deserve the comfort of others.

8.

*A*VOIDING
BURNOUT

"Taking care of our father has blown my relationship with my sister," Lauren said during her CARE-NET interview. "My children and husband are upset. I want out but I don't know how until Father dies. He has no quality of life.

"Caregiving has affected my family and my work. I am not cut out for this. My normal personality is that of a 'pleaser.' I get stressed and upset when I can't work things out. I feel as if I'm hardened, and I'm concerned about it. I don't have anyone in my family who wants to get involved. My health is going down because of stress. If I could learn how to control stress and frustration, I would be better off. I'm no good as a caregiver. . . . I want to run away."

Now listen to Faye's story, as she unburdened herself during her CARE-NET interview: "Due to the crippling effects of the disease, my father required absolutely total care. He didn't want anyone but me, and I thought I was supposed to do it all. At the time, I was self-employed, operating a small bookstore. I moved the business and my entire life to take care of him and renovated the house to meet his needs. I knew he was violently opposed to nursing-home placement, which was the only alternative. I also felt that I owed him."

Both of these women are showing the strain of caregiving— both seem to be headed toward burnout. In fact, Faye did have a caregiving breakdown of sorts. In Chapter 3, I described how she packed her bags and escaped to a motel for several hours one afternoon, leaving her severely disabled father home alone in his wheelchair.

Burnout can be dangerous to you and your loved one. When you find yourself in an acutely stressful situation over a long period of time, you may reach the limits of your ability to cope. As in Lauren's case, your health and positive relationships may be threatened. As in Faye's situation, your capacity and willingness to care for your loved one may diminish. Like both participants, you may feel the need to run. One woman in our study complained of depression and mood swings and even found herself lashing out at her frail elderly aunt as the pressure and frustration of her situation became too great for her to bear.

As damaging as it is, burnout is quite common among caregivers. Recall that in our CARE-NET survey, half of the informal caregivers reported that they are "probably experiencing burnout." And many more—85 percent—complained of feeling "just plain exhausted" at the end of the day.

It is easy to see why this is so. Burnout results from the combined effects of one's emotional dilemmas (including feelings of helplessness, guilt, and lack of recognition), family discord, and isolation. Add to that the urgency and tension caused by too many demands upon one's strength, resources, time, and energy, and you can see why many caregivers experience this sense of utter depletion.

Burnout can affect your health, motivation, attitude, and mood. It can spill over from the caregiving role to other aspects of your life. But although it can be harmful, it is not necessarily inevitable or permanent. In this chapter, I will present some strategies to help you avoid the bane of all caregivers, professional and lay alike. The first step is recognizing its signs and determining if you are suffering from its effects.

THE SIGNS OF BURNOUT

At the Inaugural Conference of the Rosalynn Carter Institute, Dr. Herbert J. Freudenberger, a clinical psychologist from New York City who has written many scholarly articles and several books on the subject, explained to us that burnout doesn't happen all at once, but, rather, it grows slowly, in stages.

At first, most caregivers go through a "honeymoon" period. They enter the caregiving relationship with a sense of idealism and hope, an eagerness to do good. But after six to eighteen months, when the situation becomes more routine and unexpected disappointments can and do occur, the stage is set.

During the second phase, the warning signs of burnout begin to become apparent. Caregivers may:

- feel less motivated.
- voice complaints about the caregiving role.
- become less efficient, putting in more hours but with poorer results.

During the third stage, caregivers experience more serious problems, including chronic physical, mental, and behavioral symptoms. Physical signs can include:

- insomnia
- headaches
- backaches
- fatigue or lethargy
- skin conditions (eczema, acne, hives)
- cardiovascular problems
- gastrointestinal symptoms or weight loss
- lingering colds

Mental signs can include:

- frustration and easily aroused irritation
- anger
- feelings of emptiness and sadness
- inability to concentrate and slowed thought
- pessimism
- a sense of being overwhelmed or overloaded
- resentment
- a loss of self-confidence and self-esteem
- depression and emotional exhaustion

These physical and mental signs can manifest themselves in one's behavior:

- Caregivers may wish to or actually try to run away. Some people become workaholics, putting in long hours at their offices, or, conversely, surrender their lives and become lost in the caregiving role.

- They may have unpleasant communications with other family members, friends, and co-workers.
- They may become "blamers."
- They may cut themselves off from others.
- They may turn to alcohol or drugs.
- They may experience sexual problems.

The participants in our CARE-NET survey responded to statements pertaining to burnout that you might find useful in determining your own state of mind. To each of the following sentences, they indicated "strongly disagree," "disagree," "agree," or "strongly agree." Where do you fit in the burnout continuum?

- I feel used up at the end of the day.
- I seem to be working harder and harder and accomplishing less and less.
- There are many days when I feel just plain exhausted.
- I am increasingly saddened and disappointed by others.
- I am experiencing physical or emotional problems that are a result of my caregiving.
- Depression seems to be an increasing problem for me.
- I feel confused when the activity of the day comes to a halt.

If you find that you are encountering many of the signs Dr. Freudenberger noted or you identify with the statements from our survey, then you are in danger of burnout. Be sure to get help for yourself. You'll find some useful suggestions later in this chapter.

WHAT CREATES BURNOUT?

According to Dr. Freudenberger, burnout is most likely to occur in situations "with no clear job-role definitions, where communication is poor, and uncertainty exists about rewards." An unpredictable or unsure decision-making process can also contribute to it. These conditions may exist in many family caregiving settings.

Although each of us and our circumstances are unique, Dr. Freudenberger also found that certain personality traits may contribute to burnout. Ironically, these are generally positive, noble attributes, but sometimes they can create situations in which one exhausts oneself:

- perfectionism and high expectations of oneself and others
- the need to work hard
- commitment, dedication, and idealism
- the need to prove oneself
- a strong goal orientation
- difficulty saying no
- difficulty delegating responsibilities to others
- self-sacrifice
- an unrealistic sense of one's limitations—seeing oneself as a "super" person
- being a "giver" rather than a "receiver"

Remember, with all of these traits, it is a question of degree. Research conducted by Drs. Merle A. Keitel, Stanley Cramer, and Michael Zevon on the spouses of cancer patients shows how significant a caregiver's feelings of helplessness can be in contributing to burnout. As they reported in the scholarly publication *Journal of Counseling and Development,* caregivers often try to fulfill all of their loved ones' needs in an effort to "fix" a problem over which they have little control. Taking over in this way helps combat their feelings of powerlessness and reduces their guilt. In the process, though, these caregivers tend to ignore their own needs. The result: burnout and, most likely, their loved ones' resentment at being made to feel totally dependent.

In our CARE-NET study, the participants' level of burnout depended on several additional factors. Predictably, caregivers who received help from others had the lowest rates, while those without assistance had the highest. In addition, those whose caregiving involved providing help with personal hygiene (bathing, dressing, bodily functions) tended to have higher rates; taking care of these needs is demanding, continuous, and relatively unrewarding. Finally, those individuals who stated that religion was only moderately important in their lives had a considerably higher rate of burnout than those who derived strength, meaning, and revitalization from their faith.

From our research, it is clear that caregivers who find some form of physical or spiritual relief are less likely to experience burnout.

WOMEN AND BURNOUT

The women caregivers in our study were more likely to express a sense of bitterness about their situation than were the men. This is not surprising when you consider that men generally assume limited responsibility in a caregiving role. Most often the full burden of caregiving falls on women. Recall that 80 percent of the lay caregivers we surveyed were women. Why is this so? In our society women have traditionally been the family "nurturers." We expect this of them.

But these days women often have multiple lifetime caregiving careers. They spend years of their lives raising children, and then usually more years caring for elderly parents and eventually ailing husbands. Sometimes these responsibilities overlap, as in the case of Lauren, who in addition to caring for her father was also parenting a developmentally disabled child.

Dr. Richard L. Edwards, dean and professor at the Mandel School of Applied Social Sciences at Case Western Reserve University, commented on women's particular obligations during the 1988 Inaugural Conference of the Rosalynn Carter Institute. "The term 'family caregiving' is somewhat misleading since family members rarely share the burdens of caregiving," he told us. "Rather, family caregiving is most often provided by one person, and most of those who provide care are women— mothers, wives, daughters, or granddaughters."

Men, according to Dr. Edwards, are more apt to offer indirect help such as financial management and home maintenance. "Men tend to assume primary caregiving responsibilities," he explained, "only when there is not a female relative available to provide such care."

Other researchers have also noted that men tend to take a more managerial role. Dr. Michael Creedon, professor of gerontology and social work at Johns Hopkins University, explained at the Fifth Annual RCI Conference, in 1993, that women almost always provide the intimate forms of care such as bathing, feeding, washing, toileting, and dressing (which our research indicates is more stressful). On the other hand, men are more apt to deal with service agencies, wills, and legal, financial, and housing issues. "Men are willing to take on managerial functions," Dr. Creedon explained, "but when it comes to direct-care services, which are much more time-consuming, the great majority of that is done by women."

Dr. Creedon spoke of women's roles in terms of baseball. "The caregiving daughter is the designated hitter for the family," he said. "It's the oldest daughter, the closest daughter, the favorite daughter, or the daughter who is going to get the house. The way in which families select their primary caregiver is mysterious. There seems to be no particular rule as to who gets this job, but there certainly is the rule that once you have it, you're stuck with it."

He went on to explain that other family members make only minor changes in their work schedules in order to help with caregiving. "In fact, when the female spouse takes on caregiving roles, male spouses make an adjustment in the order of minutes per day."

Perhaps the most stressed group of female caregivers are daughters-in-law. According to a national survey by the AARP, 14 percent of full-time employees and 8 percent of part-time employees were taking care of an elderly parent-in-law. This is significant because research strongly affirms that daughters-in-law often feel ambivalent and emotionally pressured into taking on caregiving duties for an in-law.

"When the fellow married the lady and whispered sweet nothings in her ear," Dr. Creedon said, "he almost never got around to saying, 'By the way, I also expect you to be taking care of my mother.' Very few daughters-in-law look forward to caregiving obligations toward someone whom they may or may not have gotten along very well with during the years of their marriage."

When women combine these demanding family roles with their professional lives, they are likely to become exhausted and experience burnout. Travelers Insurance Company, in a survey of its own employees, found that the average working female caregiver was engaged in caregiving activities fifteen hours a week, while the average working male caregiver was putting in only five hours. According to Dr. Creedon, other studies confirm that women devote roughly three times as many hours to caregiving responsibilities as men.

Dr. D. Patricia Gray, a professor of nursing at Georgia State University, pointed out to us at the Inaugural Conference that low self-esteem can also contribute to burnout for women. This is especially true for older women who care for their spouses in relative isolation. Family caregiving is unpaid labor. Unfortunately, in today's society, our value is frequently determined by how much money we earn. "If one is not paid for one's work," Dr. Gray explained, "then it is often assumed that the work is not valuable or valued." This may cause the women providing care to question their own sense of self-worth.

And it may undermine their ability to take care of themselves. "The predominant messages to female caregivers," Dr. Gray said, "are that everyone else is more important than self, that one's time is owed to those requiring care, and that self comes last." Such a conscientious but eventually self-defeating attitude can produce feelings of guilt, self-sacrifice, and worry. According to Dr. Gray, it can lead to a situation in which a caregiver can't even imagine putting her own needs first from time to time and taking care of herself. And, of course, if she doesn't, she will surely risk burnout.

CAREGIVERS OFFER ADVICE

While the experts have all kinds of advice about how to avoid burnout, you might find it helpful to hear from the participants in our CARE-NET study. After all, these caregivers struggle daily with the same problems you face. When we asked them, "What kind of advice would you give to lay caregivers?" the majority of their responses involved avoiding burnout. The following are representative:

- "I now know that a person must look after himself before he can be a good caregiver."
- "Never forget yourself. Get dressed up every once in a while."
- "Go to church; help your neighbors. Volunteer more. Be more involved with other people. If you tie yourself down, it can get out of hand."
- "Find out what is available in your community. Network with other care providers; give yourself dignity."
- "Make an inventory of what you need. Put your needs down on paper, then address them."
- "Take a break . . . get away from the caregiving situation from time to time."
- "How do you get help? Pay for it; demand help from family members."
- "Get the family together and explain everything. I should have said, 'I can do 1, 2, and 3 and you can do 4, 5, and 6.' "

Sissy Bowen, the young woman who co-founded the Alzheimer's support group in Americus, wrote in the group's first newsletter about her struggle to allow herself respite. Perhaps you will take comfort from her inner conflict and its resolution.

Many of us are reluctant to trust anyone else to care for our loved ones. We feel as though we are the only ones who can sufficiently provide for him or her. Moreover, many of us feel as though we are neglecting our responsibilities by allowing someone else to relieve us, even for a short time. Unfortunately, guilt is often our most prevalent emotion.

When I reluctantly hired my first sitter, I felt like many mothers must feel when they leave their newborn for the first time. I only went across the street, yet I called a dozen times, worried the entire day, and repeatedly thought to myself, I could have waited a little longer to get a sitter, and I'm just wimping out! I have since learned that what I thought was farthest from the truth.

By hiring that first sitter, I made one of the most responsible decisions of my time as a caregiver. I've learned that when I'm rested, I am a much more effective caregiver and my loved one is far better cared for. That ugly guilt is not as prominent, because I know she is being cared for by a more capable me and my entrusted sitters.

RESPITE

For many caregivers, including Sissy, temporary relief from burnout comes with respite. What is respite? It simply means getting a break from your caregiving responsibilities for a few hours or a few days. It may not eliminate all of your problems, but it can certainly make you feel better and energize you so that you can face a new day.

Respite can come in many forms. The National Federation of Interfaith Volunteer Caregivers (see Chapter 7) has established a program with volunteers trained to provide respite for Alzheimer's patients and their families, allowing primary care- givers some precious time to themselves, perhaps to do nothing more than get out in the garden for a couple of hours, if that's what they want to do. The Federation is currently working on a project to relieve caregivers of AIDS patients, as well.

Other respite programs may exist in your community. The support groups discussed in Chapter 7 can provide enormous relief by offering a refuge in which you can safely vent your frustrations and resentments while you learn useful coping skills. Housekeepers, home attendants, mobile respite pro- grams, sitters, visiting nurses, adult day-care centers (where so- cial activities, meals, and perhaps therapy are available), and day hospitals can also give you a much-needed break.

You may learn of these from the sources I have mentioned earlier, including a peer support group meeting, through your doctor's office, from a hospital social worker, from another fam- ily caregiver in your neighborhood, and also from your state's commission on aging. The National Council on Aging pub- lishes a *Directory of Adult Day Care in America* that you may find useful too (see Appendix B for the address).

OTHER HELPFUL STRATEGIES

Since each person's experiences are unique, the solutions that work for one caregiver may not work for another. I offer the following suggestions in the hope that you will find at least some of them useful and practical.

1. *Listen to your friends.* If those around you have observed a change in your behavior or demeanor, don't contradict them without first taking a minute to evaluate whether what they are saying is true. The first step in resolving burnout is recognizing that you're suffering from it. Be open to others' observations.

2. *Let go.* No one person can do it all. Acknowledge that as a human you have limitations just like everyone else. Allow others to help you; delegate responsibilities. Practice asking for help and saying no once in a while. Lower your expectations and tolerate that things might not get done perfectly; your health and well-being are more important than washing the dishes after every meal. Prioritize tasks and learn to manage your time.

3. *Focus on your loved one's strengths.* Many caregivers find it natural to worry about what their loved ones are unable to do. But allow your loved one to perform whichever activities of daily living he or she can, even if things don't get accomplished as quickly or as well as you might prefer.

4. *Learn relaxation techniques.* Some people find meditation and yoga helpful. Others use biofeedback to relieve stress, but this may not be available to you. At the risk of being repetitive, I want to stress how important it is to enjoy some kind of relaxing outlet: exercising, listening to music, gardening, reading a good book, sewing, taking a walk, or just napping. Some individuals need to vent their frustrations. In Chapter 5, I outlined some safe ways to release excess anger and tension before you reach the breaking point. Use them if you need to!

5. *Take care of your health.* Recent research has shown that stressful situations can encourage smoking, drinking, overeating, or other unhealthful practices. But if you ignore your own health, you won't be much help to your loved one. Be sure to

eat well and get enough exercise. Control unhealthful habits such as smoking or excess drinking. See the doctor for your own aches and pains. You're entitled to care and attention too.

6. *Maintain a life outside your caregiving role.* Dr. Freudenberger suggests that caregivers develop hobbies, learn new skills, and attend seminars or classes that promote personal and professional growth to prevent the caregiving role from enveloping them. Some caregivers find regular swimming useful since it provides exercise and solitude. A good hobby to take up would be photography. You could record happy times with your ill family member, and also add beauty to your days by photographing flowers or budding trees or animals in the yard.

Jimmy and I have taken up bird-watching in the last few years, and it has opened up a wonderful new interest in our lives. Buy a bird book and set up a feeder outside a window. You will be amazed at the variety of birds that will appear. I never dreamed we had cuckoos in our yard in Plains, Georgia! Under whatever circumstances, don't let go of your life.

7. *Keep a daily "burnout log."* This is another of Dr. Freudenberger's useful suggestions. Record the events that create stress in your life. After several weeks, you will be able to identify problems, evaluate the situation, and weigh possible solutions.

8. *Insist on private time.* We all need time to ourselves. Take time to do things just for you when your loved one is sleeping. Have another family member take over, if possible, or hire a sitter for a few hours, a day, or a weekend. You might find that your loved one values a change of pace or a new face.

9. *Build a caregiving team.* You don't have to face caregiving alone. Don't shy away from asking family members and close relatives to assist you, even if you don't think they will want to help. Family brainstorming sessions can be uplifting and may

result in ideas that hadn't occurred to you before. And work with your loved one's doctors, nurses, social workers, and even clergy to find solutions to your problems. Learn to trust others; they are there to help you.

10. *Rely on your sense of humor.* What better time to laugh than when your situation looks bleak? A good chuckle can get you through the worst of times. Peer support groups can be most useful in this regard. One of the things that Sybil Carter did when Jimmy's brother, Billy, was sick was write down the funny things Billy said. She has these wonderful memories now to savor, but also to share with the children, several of whom were very young when Billy died. You probably have to look for the humor in your daily activities, but try to make light of difficult situations and laugh about them (if you can!). Your tasks will be easier.

11. *Appreciate the benefits of leisure time.* Time constraints, obligations, and guilt may prevent you from enjoying any leisure time. But savoring leisure is not selfish—it is life-affirming. Assess how you spent your leisure time before you became a caregiver. How do you spend it now? Can you adapt some of your former activities to include your loved one? Movie theaters are wheelchair-accessible and wheelchairs are available at malls and airports. Reading can be enjoyable. If it's impossible to include your loved one, try to find ways to enjoy your leisure guilt-free. You deserve it.

12. *Help your loved one find a support group.* Just as you are struggling with fear, frustration, and isolation, so may the one you are caring for. A support group for him or her can provide an outlet for emotions that cannot be expressed in the home. It can also help the ill one feel less alone and helpless. Your loved one's more positive attitude can render your task less stressful

and even more enjoyable. (See Appendix B for self-help clearinghouses and organizations that sponsor support groups.)

13. *Seek professional help.* If you've tried many of these suggestions to little avail, you may benefit from seeing a counselor who specializes in stress reduction or families with chronic illnesses. A counselor may help you to ventilate negative feelings about your loved one and your caregiving experience in a safe environment. He or she can also encourage you to let go of unrealistic expectations and teach you new coping strategies.

14. *Appreciate your own efforts.* All the caregiving in the world will not save a terminally ill individual. Diseases take their own course, no matter how diligently you may provide loving care. Frustration about your powerlessness in face of the ravages of illness can contribute to your feelings of burnout. Rather than belaboring yourself for your inability to cure what is incurable, draw strength and comfort from what you can do. You can provide dignity and care and love. You cannot control the outcome. That rests in God's hands.

15. *Seek spiritual renewal.* Just as the participants in our study found solace in their faith, so may this be your primary source of help. Religious services, conversations with clergy, or individual worship can help to alleviate your stress and give you strength and inspiration.

A SHIFT IN ATTITUDE

In 1991, Dr. Rhonda J. V. Montgomery, the director of the Gerontology Center of the University of Kansas at Lawrence, came to talk to us about the joys and burdens of caregiving. Dr. Montgomery has conducted much research on aging, public policy, and family relations of older adults. She is also engaged in the design and delivery of respite services for families caring for persons with Alzheimer's disease. She is well versed in the issues surrounding burnout.

While she was conducting her research, Dr. Montgomery discovered that a proportion of the caregivers she interviewed wouldn't talk about their problems. "If you asked them about it," she explained, "they rarely brought up that caregiving was a burden. Indeed, the one thing that researchers have found is that caregivers *are* burdened. But we have been surprised at how little burden these individuals express."

Then she told the story of a gentleman whom she had visited in his home. He cared for his wife who had suffered from Alzheimer's for fifteen years. He brought Dr. Montgomery into the room where his wife slept. She was bedridden and could be fed only through tubes. But he talked to her anyway and introduced Dr. Montgomery to her.

When Dr. Montgomery asked this man about his life, he said, "Oh, this is not a trouble. This is what she would have done for me."

"Not only did this gentleman not express any burden," Dr. Montgomery explained, "but he went on to tell me about his volunteer job with the adult day-care center. There were people there that needed his help. And he wasn't unique. I kept running into more and more individuals like this."

Dr. Montgomery became curious about what made these people different. Why is it that some individuals, when faced with caregiving, feel overwhelmed by it, while others who have what appear to be equally overwhelming jobs are successful at it? What makes those people feel joy? Apparently it doesn't have much to do with the tasks required. Dr. Montgomery found caregivers like this gentleman who were immersed in total care and suffered no burnout, while others who had relatively light responsibilities were truly overwhelmed.

The difference, it seems, is attitude. "I discovered," Dr. Montgomery said, "that the people who were most successful, who were able to deal with caregiving as a joy and an opportunity, considered it a *volunteer* job. I know that given our public policy, there aren't a lot of alternatives for many people. . . . I'm not saying that caregivers have many choices, but they have a range. They have choices within limits. And if you can begin to see that you are volunteering within limits, it's helpful."

The choices may be difficult. Caregivers might have chosen their particular role to avoid guilt, or perhaps alternatives such as nursing-home placement just don't fit into their situation, but they have made choices nonetheless.

Dr. Montgomery's findings are noteworthy. We all like to have control over our lives. When caregivers view their role as voluntary, they feel in charge. They create the rules of their involvement and define what constitutes success. In fact, success can be nothing more than the ability to continue giving care. Nobody, not even other family members, can dictate to a volunteer how the job should be done.

Dr. Montgomery also reiterated that caregiving does not have to be an all-or-nothing proposition. "Those caregivers who are the most burdened and stressed feel that they must do everything. But once caregivers have come to the idea that they define how to do the caregiving, they can be a manager, they can be a helper. They don't have to do it all, and still they can be good caregivers."

This new attitude can also help you as a caregiver see other opportunities. If you recognize that there is more than one way of doing a task, you can begin to seek out support services. You can understand the value of peer groups, adult day care, and respite programs. Instead of viewing the use of these services as an admission of weakness or failure—as Sissy Bowen did when she thought, I'm just wimping out, after hiring her first sitter— you can call on the help that is available in your community so that you can continue in your caregiving role without experiencing burnout.

And that is the ultimate goal, after all, is it not?

9.

$\mathcal{D}$EALING WITH DOCTORS AND OTHER FORMAL CAREGIVERS

Formal or professional caregivers have been an important part of our lives. Jimmy's mother was a nurse, and when he was growing up, most of their close circle of friends were doctors and nurses. The suffering of those in our community was an everyday subject of conversation in his family.

Possibly because of this, and the experience with my father's illness, one of our primary interests in public life has been in health care. Jimmy and I have worked with doctors, nurses, social workers, drug abuse counselors, mental health therapists, physical therapists—the range of health-care professionals. Also, we have a family doctor whom we have been consulting for years about any aches and pains and who refers us to specialists when necessary.

Although our personal relationship with professionals has always been satisfactory, it became clear when we began our

CARE-NET study that many family caregivers have problems with the formal caregiving establishment. To gather participants, our team of researchers approached various health-related facilities in the area, asking professionals for the names of family members or others who cared for their patients at home. Surprisingly, few names were forthcoming. This was the first indication that there might be a need for better communication between professionals and their patients' caregivers, since follow-up and compliance with doctors' orders are such an important part of medical treatment.

As we conducted our survey and interviews, we found that many informal caregivers did feel that they lacked an appropriate relationship with the professionals overseeing the care of their loved ones.

Only slightly more than half of the lay caregivers we surveyed agreed or strongly agreed that all parties involved communicated effectively. When asked during the interview to describe good and bad experiences with professionals, the single most dominant issue mentioned was communication and information-sharing. Many expressed reservations about professionals listening to them or their ill family members. Ninety percent of the lay caregivers said there should be more cooperation between agencies and caregivers to provide better care. Only 58 percent agreed that formal caregivers are able and willing to help them. Frequent comments included the wish that professionals show more empathy, sensitivity, and compassion.

Faye, the woman I described in Chapter 5 who had escaped to a motel because of burnout, said, "No professionals reached out to me; I didn't know I could reach out to them." And Carla, the wife who in Chapter 6 described herself as a "benevolent manipulator," complained bitterly about her treatment:

> I had to make special arrangements to get off work for a meeting with the social worker at the hospital. When I got there, no one seemed to know anything about it. The caseworker did not show up for the appointment. I learned later that the caseworker had forgotten. I was never offered an apology and another appointment was not made. Dr. Jones . . . did not tell me anything about my husband's condition, what to expect when he came home, or what type of treatment he needed. . . . I was not involved in any discharge planning, and to my knowledge no plan of care was made for my husband.

Carla's experience represents the worst of what can happen, but it's not the only kind of poor communication that can occur. One man was angry because the doctors insisted on going through the social workers instead of communicating directly with him about his ailing daughter. Another urged that health professionals listen to the family caregivers. "Accept the lay caregiver as the 'professional' in the specific situation," he said. "They know more about the individual than anyone else." One caregiver noted that her pharmacist helped her more than anyone. Among other comments:

> "Doctors need to be told that the emotional and physical are both important."
> "TLC will go further than all the medication you can give."
> "Respect the informal caregiver."
> "Treat others as you would be treated."
> "I don't want to be patronized."

Negative attitudes from health professionals can add to caregivers' stress and sense of impotence and isolation. This may be harmful to the patients, whose physical and emotional well-being are tied to their relationships with professionals. Ideally, professionals, family caregivers, and patients should act as a team, dedicated to providing the best care possible. Trust, comfort, and respect are the watchwords.

Why are there so often problems between formal and informal caregivers? Some of it has to do with training, some with burnout, some with ethics, and some simply with human nature.

DIFFICULTIES IN THE DOCTOR-CAREGIVER RELATIONSHIP

There are many reasons why lay caregivers' interactions with the health-care establishment are unsatisfactory. Perhaps the first and most obvious is that physicians focus on the doctor-patient relationship, not the doctor-*caregiver* one. As a caregiver, you think of your loved one as a *person* first; your doctor probably sees him or her as a *patient* first. Medical doctors are trained to think in terms of physical abnormality and dysfunction of the *body*. Patients' emotional needs and their relationship to a spouse or family may be outside doctors' line of vision. As one professional in our CARE-NET study explained, "Sometimes doctors aren't aware of needs. There is a big gap."

Second, doctors are highly motivated to cure and heal. They have devoted their lives to this pursuit, and it is most satisfying for them to do so. But certain illnesses can't be cured or healed. For years, I had a recurring pain in my right side. My appendix had already been removed; my doctor put me through every test he could think of to detect the problem. He could find nothing wrong. I complained about it until, eventually, whenever I went for my annual checkups, the doctor would say, "Is there anything else bothering you other than your right side?" Since he couldn't cure my pain, he lost interest —not in me, but in this particular problem. If doctors lose interest in a patient's case, imagine how they might feel about the caregiver.

In addition, whereas a general practitioner may be well acquainted with one's family and the medical histories and needs of all of its members, a specialist will most likely focus solely on the ill individual, or just on the disease process itself. The caregiver's needs and concerns become secondary to the physical aspects of the illness.

Also, some doctors simply are uncomfortable treating patients and their families as partners. Dr. Harold H. Benjamin, founder of the Wellness Community, a nationwide network of psychosocial support groups for cancer patients and their families, explains in his book, *From Victim to Victor,* that while most physicians look forward to having the patient act as a partner, others "because of temperament or training, can only interact with patients as a parental figure."

Physicians who view themselves in this way are less likely to share the responsibility of care, discuss treatment options, or answer questions and accept input from patients and their caregivers. They are used to giving orders and having others follow them. They may be brusque, use confusing medical jargon, and interrupt the patient or caregiver as he or she discloses important information.

Indeed, some professional caregivers in our study admitted that they made little effort to connect with lay caregivers. One social worker said ruefully, "As professionals, we have a tendency to feel a bit superior. We don't give the client and family sufficient credit to tell us what they need." Another said, "Being a supervisor, you think about what the client needs, and you forget about what the caregiver is giving." These and other formal caregivers seemed to imply that family involvement, if too intense, could "muddy the works." In the process, the caregiver may be left out of the loop.

It is also true that ill family members and their caregivers may have differing coping styles. According to Dr. Benjamin, some people who are sick want all the information they can get from professionals, while others want only to be told what to do. Some want to know all the options so they can decide on the course of treatment themselves, whereas others rely strictly on the doctor to decide. Some ask questions, record answers, and bring family members into the examining room while others don't. The family caregivers' relationships with professionals, therefore, may also depend on the patients' preferences.

PROFESSIONALS ARE OVERWHELMED, TOO

Many formal caregivers realize that there are problems in their relationships with informal caregivers but feel so swamped that they can't cope with them. From the 256 professionals who answered questionnaires and 98 interviews we conducted for our CARE-NET study, it is clear that many are quite overwhelmed by their workloads. Seventy-five percent said they were exhausted at the end of the day. More than half said they did not have sufficient time to consult with families regarding how they might assist with the care of the patients.

Professionals complained most often about bureaucratic administrative duties and "too much paperwork." In fact, 61 percent said that these kept them from being effective on the job. One formal caregiver said, "We feel ourselves getting bogged down with pencil and paper rather than patients. There is never enough time. I have constant interruptions."

Emotional factors may be at work, too. Being a formal caregiver can be quite stressful. A psychiatric nurse said, "The work is demanding; people don't realize how much it takes of our personal life. It takes a lot of energy to give so intensely to people." And a drug abuse counselor, nearing burnout herself, stated:

> I'm overworked and underpaid. There's a great imbalance. No one seems to care about my breaking point. There are too few workers to handle the number of clients. I have too much responsibility—I handle one hundred clients by myself. I need some acknowledgment; I don't get many strokes. I only have so much to give.

It's easy to see how a professional in such a state would have a hard time being available to anyone!

As with any relationship, however, it takes two to tango. For all of their goodwill, lay caregivers are not blameless. As Dr. Benjamin explains, "A medical degree does not bestow sainthood or unlimited patience, and a physician cannot be expected to act forever as a caring friend and confidant to an overly demanding, hostile, and angry patient." The same, of course, could be said of a family caregiver, whose negative demeanor might diminish a professional's responsiveness. After all, professionals have feelings, too.

While most formal caregivers in our study were quite respectful of family members' roles in providing care, some had complaints of their own that may shed some light on their behaviors and attitudes toward informal caregivers. Indeed, their comments split between the families' lack of involvement and their overinvolvement. Some formal caregivers felt that families were not contributing enough to the total care process; others felt that families should back off and let the professionals do their jobs. Here are some of their comments:

"Families are reluctant to get involved with treatment; a family should be ready to face commitment."

"Some families are too caring and can't detach, while others aren't caring enough and can't relate to the patient's needs."

"Families are not familiar with how to care for their relatives. Some families look for problems."

"The main reason that patients come back [to the hospital]: they fail to follow the agreed plan and stop harmful activity. Families assume responsibility for care, then fail to do so."

"The families feel that the professional is interfering; the families see the professional as an outsider."

"The family needs to realize the duties and limits of the professional. Professionals can't do everything."

"Some families try to do too much without the doctor's orders."

"Parents sometimes don't see the necessity of following the instructions of the professional."

"One client calls constantly."

"Families will not try to learn what technical and caregiving information is available."

"The family gets very emotionally involved, whereas the staff has 230 different families. Family members must understand that time is of the essence."

"Sometimes family members are angry, tired, guilt-ridden. There are misunderstandings."

Apparently so.

WHAT'S A CAREGIVER TO DO?

While it's disheartening to see the difficulties in the professional–family caregiver relationship, there are steps one can take to ease the situation and avoid power struggles. The following suggestions gleaned from experts and the formal and informal caregivers in our survey may help:

Discuss your role with your loved one and the professionals. Although you are caring for your loved one, you are not the identified patient. Professionals have legal responsibilities toward the one who is sick, not toward you! Psychiatrists and psychologists, for example, cannot share information about a person's diagnosis or give a progress report unless the one being treated agrees to it in writing. Their code of ethics requires that they keep the patient's sessions private. Any breach of confidentiality could be the cause of a lawsuit (and even the professional's loss of license), but more important, it could seriously damage the therapeutic relationship and interfere with the delivery of care.

That being the case, discuss with your family member the

kind and degree of your involvement. Then let the professional know whether you'll participate in all medical decisions. If your loved one feels comfortable with the idea, it is all right to go into the examining room. If not, he or she can inform the professional that you would like to be called in after the examination is complete but before the results are given, so you can be part of the total care process. Most doctors will oblige such a request, but may not take it upon themselves to include you without the patient's say-so.

If the one you are caring for is a minor, mentally impaired, or otherwise unable to communicate wishes to the professionals, make plain that you will be the caregiver when you leave the doctor's office, hospital, or clinic. Explain that you would like to be included in a discharge meeting and informed of treatment plans, changes in medications and the potential side effects, dietary restrictions, or other factors that might be important.

Designate a quarterback. Several professionals may be involved in your loved one's care and you may find it confusing and difficult to deal with so many individuals who seem to be acting independently. In an effort to save everyone's energy, you might find it helpful to do what Jimmy and I have done for ourselves. Ask one physician, for example your internal medicine specialist or cardiologist, to coordinate care and become the conduit of all information to you. This has worked for us and should simplify your life and reduce stress since you will need to focus on only one relationship.

Be involved but be prepared. One of the professionals in our study suggested that family members need to understand how the system works so they can focus on what is really important. Another added that they need to educate themselves enough to comprehend what the professional recommends and follow instructions. "If they disagree," she explained, "it's their responsibility to ask why and what will take place in treatment." And another urged, "Be inquisitive. Don't give up if you don't get the answers you need. Keep going. Find someone else to ask." When you educate yourself about the illness and the circumstances involved, you will be able to discuss options intelligently.

The first source of information will most likely be the primary professional caring for your ill family member. If you have questions you would like answered, write them down and bring your list along to the office or meeting. As you have seen from our survey, most professionals are quite busy—if not harried—and may not have the time to wait as you organize your thoughts on the spot. Your loved one, too, may have questions. You might wish to combine them with yours to save time. This way the professional won't have to repeat answers. Besides, this is a stressful time for all of you. The less you leave to chance, the more in control you will feel.

Some questions you might want to ask the doctor are:

What causes this disease?
What is the prognosis?
Will surgery be required?
Can the disease be controlled with treatment?
What kind of treatment?
How often will the treatments be needed, and for how long?
Are there options as far as treatment is concerned?
Is the treatment available here in our community?

What are the risks involved in the treatment?

What kind of medication will be needed?

What are the side effects?

Will we need to call in other specialists for consultation?

Is there anything we can do to speed up recovery?

Are there others in the community with the same diagnosis with whom we could talk?

Are there support groups in our community?

Who can we call if we can't reach you in case of an emergency?

Can we care for our loved one at home?

What kind of services or supplies will we need?

If the professional gives you information you cannot understand, ask that it be explained in simpler, less technical terms. Sometimes it is helpful for a physician to draw a picture of the problem or demonstrate using a three-dimensional model. Be persistent. If you misunderstand the professional's instructions, you may make a mistake in medicine dosage or you may follow an improper treatment plan that can have negative consequences. Take notes on the professional's responses. In the stress of an exam, you might forget or confuse explanations or instructions.

If you have many concerns to discuss—too many, in fact, to fit into the time the professional has allotted—then make a separate consultation appointment. You may also find it helpful to search out more information at the library or bookstore. Today, many books are available that explain various maladies and their treatment to the lay public. Just as a general reference, on a bookshelf at home, I have a medical dictionary, a psychiatric dictionary, and a family medical guide. In addition,

I have a book describing dysfunctions of the thyroid, since I have a chronic thyroid problem.

For further information concerning a particular illness, check with those organizations listed in Appendix B. They may have brochures and other information they can share with you. You'll also find helpful books listed—both general and disease-specific—in Appendix B.

Maintain reasonable expectations. Several professional caregivers in our survey noted that they don't have all the answers, especially when it comes to diseases that are not fully understood. As one explained, "Families need to realize the limits of the professionals." On the other hand, another complained, "Patients don't take care of themselves after they leave the doctor. Sometimes they take too much or not enough of their medication."

It is not uncommon for people to feel intimidated by a physician's education and power. In fact, some informal caregivers seem afraid to "impose" on the doctor with their problems. "He's a busy person," they say with great deference. "I don't want to bother him." Yet caregivers must make sure their ill family members are getting all the professional care they need. How can they do that without "bothering" the doctor from time to time?

Underlying these issues is the larger question of realistic expectations. What should you count on from the professionals with whom you are dealing? What should they anticipate from you? The following are reasonable expectations and responsibilities that you assume when you agree to be a caregiver.

As a lay caregiver, you should:

- Make sure your loved one follows the professional's instructions. A "medication box," for example, can aid in organizing pills. I have a small plastic one that holds a week's supply of pills, with small compartments for each day. When I was diagnosed with a thyroid condition, this helped me finally get into the habit of daily dosages. Taking medicine as prescribed is most important! Unfortunately, many people suffer and even die needlessly each year because they don't comply with their doctor's orders.

- Give the professional all the information you have about the symptoms and condition of the one you are caring for, and all medications or therapies he or she is taking. It may help to write these down along with the questions you wanted answered.

    When my mother was in the hospital recently, a nurse made a chart for her, listing her medicines, how much she should take each day, and when to take them. My mother keeps it on a bulletin board in her kitchen, so it is always handy. Also, on occasion, when she has to go to the emergency room, we take it along. It saves explaining about medication to the doctor on duty.

- Contact the professional if you're concerned about changes in your loved one's condition. Don't attempt to "play doctor" yourself.

- Be respectful of the professional's time. Honor your appointments, give twenty-four-hour notice if you must cancel, and call during office hours whenever possible. Reserve weekend or evening calls for emergencies only.

- Understand that your loved one is not the only patient in the professional's practice. Unless it's an emergency, the doctor may not get back to you until the end of the day.

- Be as honest as you can about what you need and expect from the professional.
- Inform the professional when seeking another opinion.
- Recognize that the professional may not have all the answers.
- Express your gratitude to professionals for their care, help, and understanding. They are human, too.

The National Family Caregivers Association suggests in their fall 1993 newsletter, *Take Care!*, that you learn the routine at your doctor's office and/or hospital so you can make the system work for you. Try to see the professionals as allies. "Separate your anger and sense of impotence about not being able to help your loved one as much as you would like from your feelings about the doctor. Remember, you are both on the same side."

And what should you reasonably expect from the professionals you're working with? The National Family Caregivers Association made the following recommendations.

Professionals should:

- Recognize that family members want to be part of the care team.
- Be forthright in giving the facts of the situation in understandable language but without patronizing.
- Think about how practical their advice is and consider its effect on the rest of the family. Instructions may be medically sound, but can they be carried out?
- Be sure that caregivers understand the potential side effects of medications and treatments.
- Respect the right of the patient and the caregiver to think about and make their own medical decisions.

- Ask how the caregiver is doing from time to time. "A touch of the hand goes a long way."
- Be attentive, especially when a caregiver is sharing intimate feelings.
- Be aware of where they impart information to the caregiver. The privacy of an office is far superior to a busy hallway or waiting room.

Caregivers should also expect professionals to be respectful of their time and burdens, return phone calls as soon as possible, and listen to their concerns without interrupting. It's common courtesy that they do so.

Confront your problems with professionals. If you are having trouble communicating with formal caregivers, you may feel stressed and upset. But perhaps more detrimental, you may harbor unexpressed resentments that can interfere with your caregiving and ultimately with your loved one's health. Clearly, this is to be avoided.

So how do you get through to a professional caregiver who seems too busy to give you the time of day? The first step is to make your needs known. Call and ask for an appointment. During your meeting, express your feelings and needs frankly. Try to avoid blaming, which can create defensiveness. Be as specific as possible. As one professional in our study put it, "Don't be afraid to ask for help." And another added, "Don't be too proud." You are the consumer; you're paying for the professional's attention.

If the formal caregiver really hears your concerns and responds to them, you can expect a change in behavior that will be beneficial for all of you. If not, you may feel the situation warrants your finding a different professional to take over the case. That, of course, may depend on the state of mind and ability of the ill family member to make such an important decision with you as well as the availability of other competent professionals in your community.

FINDING ANOTHER DOCTOR

It may be difficult to find another doctor if you live in a small town. This is especially true if all of the physicians know and support one another; they are sometimes reluctant to take on a colleague's patient. You may have to go to a neighboring or distant larger city in order to locate someone. This might prove to be difficult or even ill-advised. If your loved one requires immediate medical attention from time to time, a sixty-mile drive might be out of the question. If your community has many resources, you may be successful in locating a more compassionate and understanding professional.

Jimmy and I recently dealt with finding a new doctor for my mother, who lives in Plains. Her primary physician is in Atlanta, but since Plains is more than a hundred miles away, Mother sees a local doctor from time to time. Recently her local doctor moved to Florida. This presented us with a real dilemma. Not only did her doctor's departure affect her emotionally, but we wondered how we would find another physician. Mother asked for recommendations from her friends. Many of them had been seeing the same doctor and were also searching for a new one. Our best advice came from the administrator of the Methodist retirement and nursing home in Americus. He referred Mother to a new doctor.

How do you choose a new doctor? Ask friends and relatives for names of those to contact. They or your pastor may know someone suffering from the same disease who can advise you. There may also be a support group in your community that could make recommendations whose names you should be able to find listed in the telephone book. Or a facility like the one Jimmy and I turned to can be most helpful. Other professionals whom you see regularly in your community, such as your dentist, can give you advice. Your state and county medical association are good resources too, as are university medical schools. And the organizations such as the American Cancer Society and the American Heart Association listed in Appendix B may provide help.

Sometimes it is wise to seek a new doctor to get a second opinion. Insurance companies often require you to do so, or you and your ill family member may feel the need yourselves. Experts at times are unsure about a diagnosis or a treatment plan; some physicians respond aggressively, recommending surgery or other invasive treatments, while others are more conservative, taking a wait-and-see approach or prescribing medication. Many patients and their families want to be absolutely sure of the diagnosis before they take action. You are always within your rights to have a fresh evaluation of the problem.

I know from personal experience how important a second opinion is. Robert, one of our relatives, had prostate cancer. He received the recommended treatment but soon after, his leg started hurting in spots. His urologist told him that the cancer had metastasized and sent him to a neighboring town for a series of treatments. Several areas on the leg were affected. When one area cleared up, Robert asked for more treatment on the others. This time he was told that the cancer had spread too far; it didn't make sense to continue treatment. The best that could be done for him would be just to make him as comfortable as possible. In effect, the doctors indicated that Robert was dying.

It was at this point that his frantic wife called us. We made arrangements for Robert to go the National Cancer Institute, where, amazingly, he learned that the cancer had not spread at all! His former doctors had been mistaken. Today, Robert is healthy, leading a productive life.

You may feel awkward about seeking a second opinion. Some individuals believe they are insulting a physician's integrity if they request outside confirmation. Or they're afraid the professional will retaliate in some way! But doctors are used to this. Most will not take offense—and if they do, you might want to question their good intentions.

When you identify another doctor, let the office staff know that you are bringing in your ill family member for a "consultation." They will then understand that you are looking for a second opinion. Be sure to obtain and take with you medical records, X-rays, and any other pertinent information for the new doctor to see. These belong to the patient, and one can simply request them. This will spare you the expense of duplicate tests.

After the second opinion you may decide that you need further input, especially if this doctor's evaluation differs from the first one you received. Some families only feel comfortable after receiving three or four outside opinions. In the end, you may decide to continue treatment with the initial physician, or you may believe that a different course of action would be more beneficial. But whatever the decision, you and your loved one will feel that you have done everything you can to learn about and deal with the problem. And that should give you both some sense of peace.

MAKING IT WORK

It is possible for formal and informal caregivers to work together for the benefit of those who are sick. Today, with CARE-NET, we are making that a reality in our corner of Georgia. And others have been successful at it, as well. All it takes is willingness and a plan.

Joyce, one of the professionals in our study, described a mental health program with which she was involved. The center where Joyce works decided to put more focus on the family. "We didn't involve the family in the process as much as we should but we are now recognizing what an important role they play in the situation," she said.

The professionals developed a training program for family members. It lasted eight weeks and covered a specific topic each week. "The program was wonderful," Joyce said. "The people were starved for information. We had no idea it would go over so well. Many people attended all eight sessions."

Family members learned that professional support was just a phone call away. "They need to know that someone is there twenty-four hours a day—at the time of crisis this is critical. Crises don't always come between 8:00 A.M. and 5:00 P.M., Monday through Friday." The lay caregivers also learned what to expect from the patient, the doctor, and the clinic. "They go into caregiving blind," Joyce explained. The program attempted to correct that situation. It was so successful, the families formed a support group to which the mental health center now refers other lay caregivers.

But learning and benefits did not flow in only one direction. "When we were doing the series," Joyce said, "we [professionals] found that we were asking the family caregivers for advice. Instead of them being on one side of the fence, and us on the other, we removed the fence and got together to find the best ways to help the client."

Now, isn't that the way the system should work, for the well-being of all?

10.

$\mathcal{I}$NSTITUTIONALIZATION? ANSWERING THE DIFFICULT QUESTION

Edna and Steven are the parents of one of my friends. After fifty-three years of marriage, Edna suffered a debilitating stroke. It left her somewhat confused and with weakness on her left side. Following a stay in the hospital and several weeks at a rehabilitation clinic, she was deemed ready to go home. Edna was able to walk with a walker and could carry on a relatively reasonable conversation, but she was no longer able to take care of her personal needs or her household.

Steven took her home and immediately hired Bianca, an attendant, to care for her eight hours a day. Bianca shopped, cooked, and cleaned. She bathed Edna, went on walks with her, and became a companion as well as an employee. A physical therapist came to the home several times a week to help Edna relearn the use of her weakened limbs.

The family had barely adjusted to Edna's altered state when, two years after the first stroke, she experienced a second. Unfortunately, this one was much more devastating, causing her to behave as if she were psychotic. She hallucinated. She screamed. She thrashed around in the hospital bed so much that the nurses had to use soft restraints to prevent her from severely bruising herself and breaking her fragile bones. She required medication to control these symptoms and the tendency to have seizures. She became incontinent.

Now Steven was faced with a more difficult decision. Could he bring his wife home from the hospital? Her bizarre, agitated behavior upset and frightened him. In his late seventies himself, he feared that he would not be able to tolerate it or to keep to the rigid medication schedule Edna required. Bianca or someone else would have to live in his home day and night. His son and daughter-in-law could help, but only to a degree. Their preoccupation with their children, careers, and financial obligations made it unlikely that either would take over Edna's care.

After struggling for several months, during which Edna resided in a convalescent hospital, Steven found a solution that suited him and his family. He located a residential facility for Edna where a registered nurse was on duty. Each of the eight patients at the home had her own furnished room and bath. All had some brain dysfunction but were ambulatory. The women ate together. They watched television together in the living room and spent warm afternoons outside on the patio surrounded by rose bushes and morning glories. It was a comfortable, safe, clean environment and Edna did well there.

Steven visited his wife daily, usually around lunchtime. He made sure she ate, then he cleaned her dentures and held her hand as she slipped into her afternoon nap. On weekends, holidays, and family birthdays, Steven or his son picked up Edna and took her home for several hours. Although she couldn't orient herself to time or place (she didn't know, for example, that she was not living "at home" anymore), with the aid of medication she was able to carry on relatively appropriate conversations for short periods of time. She took pleasure in visits with her children and grandchildren but had lost much of her memory.

Then, almost like clockwork, after another two-year interval, a third stroke hit. This time, with the exception of her head and one arm, Edna became totally paralyzed. She lost most of her ability to focus or speak. Her days were spent curled in the fetal position, staring at the wall or the ceiling.

After an extended hospital stay, during which her condition stabilized, Steven attempted to take her back to the residential facility. It was no use. She was too disabled to live there. And so he put Edna in a nursing home, where she remains today. Steven continued to visit her daily until his doctor advised him to take a few days off each week—it was just too depressing for him and too taxing on his heart.

Now Edna hovers somewhere between life and death—unable to live life fully and unable to die. Sometimes when her family visits they cannot rouse her from her drug-induced sleep. Sometimes she stares blankly, with no recognition. And sometimes a faint sign of consciousness flutters through her eyes. She holds out an emaciated hand and whispers, "I love you," almost inaudibly, leaving her family to despair over how much she understands about her condition and her whereabouts.

A VERY PERSONAL DECISION

Steven's decision to institutionalize his wife came gradually, over time, as her condition worsened. It was a decision not lightly taken but agonized over, step by step. Like many family caregivers, he felt guilty that he had relinquished his wife's care to others. Often he felt like a failure. But he knew that caring for his wife at home would cost him his own life. At his age, he just couldn't do it. The best he could manage was to find the most humane care possible, and then visit Edna every day. Even if she didn't understand where she was or what had happened to her, he did not want her to feel that he had abandoned her.

In truth, only a minority—about 20 percent—of the families in our country make the decision Steven did to institutionalize their disabled loved ones. (Actually, this could be a blessing, since the nation's health-care system would be strained to bursting if everyone chose institutionalization over home care.) The caregivers we surveyed in our CARE-NET study fit right in with the national trend. Thirty-eight percent cared for their ill family members in their own homes, whereas 41 percent provided assistance in the home of the sick one. Only 21 percent availed themselves of institutional care.

Is institutionalization, then, inherently good or bad? I think it is unwise to make a value judgment on this question. Each family must make that decision based on the disabilities and preferences of the one requiring care, on financial considerations, the facilities available in the community, their own health, their feelings of guilt, and the resources for their individual strength and renewal. The choice is very personal. Moving an Alzheimer's patient who no longer recognizes anyone would have more of an effect on the caregiver than on the care recipient. It's up to the family to decide what they can tolerate.

The family may want to involve others in the decision, including friends, doctors, social workers, and the clergy. Sometimes the person facing possible institutionalization may become resistant and resentful toward family members who advocate the move. But after deliberation, when it appears that institutionalization is for the best, the disabled one might accept the proposal. It is an important and sensitive decision, and everyone should participate with as much consideration and tact as possible.

To determine if institutionalization is right for your circumstances, you might want to ask yourself the following questions:

- Does my disabled family member need round-the-clock care?
- Does my loved one have a long-term illness that does not require hospitalization for acute care?
- Does my loved one need my assistance with the activities of daily living such as walking, bathing, dressing, shopping, food preparation, and going to the toilet?
- Am I, as a family caregiver, still able to continue providing proper care and attention? And if I am unable, can someone else in the family take over for me?

Entering a nursing home, of course, will be a major life transition for your loved one. It will mean a loss of independence, a change in lifestyle, the deprivation of home, possessions, and privacy. Ill individuals often miss their familiar habits and routines. Many experience a period of depression after making this difficult move. It might be helpful for you to know that one of my friends, who operates several nursing homes and has observed residents entering for many years, says that individuals adjust better when they enter "a little bit before they need to."

Taking all of these things into consideration, a nursing facility is still a viable and sometimes necessary option—and a not altogether unfavorable one. To the contrary, many who enter nursing homes find a new life for themselves: they make new friends, have new experiences, are entertained, and have many activities to keep them occupied such as crafts, games, and socializing.

There is a story about an elderly widower in Plains that illustrates the point so perfectly. Mr. Wells lived on the same street as my mother, and after his wife died, Mother and others on their street cooked his meals and ran errands for him. He was too feeble to get out much. Everyone encouraged him to move to the Plains Convalescent Home, where he would be cared for. He wouldn't go and continued to live alone for many years. Finally he got very sick and had to be taken to the home—still against his wishes, but it was necessary.

Mr. Wells had a fig tree in his backyard, and he had always enjoyed the figs. One day a neighbor noticed that the tree was full of ripe fruit and went to the convalescent home to see if Mr. Wells wanted to go to his house and pick some of them. Mr. Wells's immediate reply was "No! They might not let me come back here!"

FAMILY CAREGIVERS' OPINIONS

When we asked the lay caregivers in our survey how they would proceed if they could no longer care for their ill family members, we received a variety of answers. Many expressed a great deal of anxiety about the changes that would take place. "I would worry myself to death," one caregiver said. "It would devastate me and my family," another added. "It's difficult to talk about," said a third. "I would feel guilty. It would destroy Mother."

Others expressed concerns about their loved one's survival. They believed no one could deliver care as well or as willingly as they had. "I do not feel my father would survive long without my assistance," one caregiver said. Added another, "I would be very unhappy and worried for a long time about whether others were doing as good a job." And a third said:

> After the heart failure and the stroke, I decided to keep Father at home and not place him in a nursing home. I decided that how long Father lived depended on home care. The money is there for a nursing home, but I believe what I am doing is right.

To these and many more caregivers in our survey, institutionalization seemed anathema.

Still, a small number of participants expressed a sense of release and even peace at the thought of relinquishing care. One caregiver said, "I would worry about my mother's care, but I would also feel relief." Another said, "I wouldn't grieve myself to death. I've done all I could do." "I would be fine," said a third. And one caregiver even admitted that she would visit her children and go to Disney World after she had institutionalized her father.

ON LETTING GO

It is one thing to reach a decision, but it may be quite another to let go. Most family caregivers have such ambivalent feelings about institutionalization that they find it difficult to release their loved one. Sissy Bowen, the young woman who formed an Alzheimer's support group in Americus, described in a letter to me her internal conflict as she made the decision to institutionalize her grandmother, "GaSara":

I've spent the greater part of the last year searching, deep within and around me, for the acceptance I need to place GaSara in the Manor. I have found that acceptance, embraced it entirely, and have spent many weeks dreaming and planning for the life I so look forward to reclaiming. . . . To think that after four and a half years, I can go to the store, the bank, for a walk, or to Paris, and I don't have to leave a number or call when I go to an unexpected destination . . . or to have a home to call my own, these are wonderful concepts. . . .

I know in my heart that I (with the obvious Power of God) have given GaSara the very best life she could have had in these years, dealing with a disease from Hell that only gets worse. I know that if I had not come here, if she didn't first suffer some fatal tragedy as a result of her decline, she would have been placed in a nursing home . . . long before it was ever necessary. I've given her life worth living despite her coping with a disease about dying. . . .

I am so tired. I'm physically and emotionally exhausted. I must rest and I cannot give that to myself until GaSara is gone. I have prayed so much that God would take her from this place entirely, that she would never have to go to the Manor, but it looks as though that's not in His plan. I accept that. "It's one thing to know, and another to respond accordingly." Despite total acceptance that she must go, I still NEVER WANTED HER TO GO into a nursing home. I accept it, but I HATE IT.

Other caregivers may wait until they are at the breaking point or until a dangerous situation develops before they make the commitment. The father of one of Sissy's friends "let go" of his wife when he realized that her body was alive but her mind was dead. And during her CARE-NET interview, Victoria described how she reached the conclusion that her father, who suffered from dementia, required the more structured environment of a nursing home:

> Two incidents made me decide to do something. The first happened at two o'clock one morning when Papa was downstairs slamming things around. I found all of the doors unlocked and some of them open. The next morning, I found some things on the front porch and I knew then that Papa had been outside during the night. About four days later, I took my eyes off of him in his rocking chair for about twenty minutes, and found him across the street, picking Mr. Jackson's apples. He had crossed that busy street during rush hour. These incidents told me that I had to do something.

TAKING HALF MEASURES

Institutionalization is not necessarily an all-or-nothing proposition. There are other options that can relieve some of the pressure without removing the patient totally from a family environment.

Adult day care, for example, can be a way station. It gives the family respite and enables the sick one to get out among others and socialize. Our neighbor Betty Godwin, a registered nurse, recently opened such a day-care center in Americus. Some of the individuals who go there are independent people; they come in to play cards and get a meal. Others are more disabled, like Florence, who experienced brain damage after an automobile accident and is totally immobile in a wheelchair. Her husband has taken care of her for years. He couldn't desert her. She had been a good mother and had raised their children. After the mishap the doctors said that Florence would never show any emotion again. But Betty has gotten her to laugh, and Florence's husband has marveled over it.

Another option is community care, in which one hires a private agency to help care for the elderly, frail individual in the home. These programs can provide transportation to the doctor, visiting nurses, personal care, help with meal preparation, grocery shopping, and other chores.

The New York Times recently reported on one such comprehensive program in Columbia, South Carolina. At Palmetto Senior Care, eligible participants spend several days every week at a day-care center where their medical and social needs are assessed by a team of doctors, social workers, nurses, therapists, pharmacists, and nutritionists. The case of Rosa Alston, a double amputee, was highlighted in the article by *Times* correspondent Tamar Lewin:

Palmetto social workers helped Mrs. Alston find and move into an apartment that she could navigate in her wheelchair with the prosthesis on her right leg. On Mondays and Fridays, Palmetto sends an aide to clean the apartment and to help her bathe. On Tuesdays and Thursdays, the Palmetto van takes Mrs. Alston to the program's day center, where she plays Bingo, makes crafts, eats lunch, leads a Bible discussion group, and is monitored for her diabetes and other health problems.

When necessary, Palmetto doctors make house calls. And when Mrs. Alston's dog, Skippy, got fleas, Palmetto paid to remove them.

Comprehensive programs like this exist in eight cities around the country, including San Francisco (the originator); Rochester, New York; New York City; and East Boston. Participants sign over their Medicare and Medicaid payments to the program and receive all services, including medical care and prescriptions, free of charge. Community care costs less than traditional nursing-home placement, and though there may not be such a comprehensive program in your community, there may be centers that offer some of the services mentioned.

Betty Godwin's day-care program in Americus, for instance, offers services other than those you would expect in a day program. She provides in-home respite care, in-home personal care, cleaning, meal preparation, and errand service. She recently told me of taking a client to see her niece in a neighboring town, and she even took one client around the golf course in a golf cart so that she could be with her husband while he played!

You might also choose a group residential facility, as Steven did. Several participants in our study who cared for emotionally disturbed or mentally retarded youngsters found these homes valuable once their children reached adulthood. One father even helped build one in his community. Group homes are also less expensive than nursing-home care, but the disabled one must be ambulatory to live there.

Finally, you might even use a nursing home on a short-term basis, if you must travel, or simply for respite. I described earlier how Jimmy's mother, Miss Lillian, spent several weeks in Magnolia Manor (the Methodist retirement and nursing home in Americus) after a fall. She needed physical therapy as she recovered from a broken hip, and it was too difficult for her to get into or out of a car twice a day for the trip to the rehabilitation clinic. We visited her regularly while she was there, and she enjoyed the experience. The decision to enter the facility, in which we all participated, was easy for her to accept— mainly because it was temporary, not permanent.

And nursing homes were not foreign to her. Some years earlier, as a registered nurse, Miss Lillian had helped to open and run a nursing home in Blakely, Georgia. What surprised her most about that adventure were the romances that took place among the elderly citizens there!

THREE LEVELS OF CARE

Do you assume that all nursing-home care is alike? That is not the case. Actually, there are three levels of care provided within most institutions. Depending on your loved one's condition, you would choose from the following:

Skilled nursing care. This is for those who need intensive, round-the-clock medical attention from a registered nurse.

Intermediate nursing care. When individuals aren't ill enough to meet the medical criteria for skilled care, they may qualify for intermediate care. They still receive twenty-four-hour supervision and nursing assistance.

Custodial care. This is for individuals who need room and board and personal help, but do not require medical or health services.

The physician and the nursing-home administrator will help you determine what kind of care is right for your family member.

WHAT YOU SHOULD LOOK FOR IN A NURSING HOME

You may have a lot of time to research nursing homes. Or, as with many families, you may find that placement is necessary following a hospital stay when your loved one's condition has worsened to the point that home care is no longer possible. In that case, you may be forced to make a hurried selection. It is wise, therefore, to have in mind some guidelines to help you determine whether a facility is acceptable.

Pamela Cody, a nursing-home marketing and admissions director and the founder of the Alzheimer's Disease and Related Disorders Association in Tallahassee, Florida, covers what you should look for in an institution in the *Florida Caregivers Handbook.* Let me share some of her insights with you here.

Ms. Cody's advice is to visit as many facilities as possible in your community, and use your power of observation. Here are some questions you might ask the administrator or yourself:

1. *How is the facility rated?* Most states license nursing homes and rate them as excellent, adequate, fair, or conditional. The license and rating should be prominently displayed. An excellent rating indicates that the home offers quality care, coupled with stimulating activities, in a clean, safe environment. If your state does not specify ratings (Georgia does not), it does require thorough, and usually unannounced, inspections of facilities. Look for the inspection results, which should be posted along with the license.

"Keep in mind that appearances can be deceiving," Cody writes. "A lavish facility may not necessarily signal good resident care."

2. *What is the quality and stability of the staff?* A nursing home should employ registered nurses, licensed practical nurses, and nurses' aides. They should work around the clock, usually in eight-hour shifts. The home should also have a doctor or medical director on staff or on call who is present for emergencies and routinely examines the patients. Family physicians can also make calls monthly or more frequently, as the patient's condition warrants. You should be able to discuss your concerns with the medical director. Look for someone who is warm and friendly toward patients and family members.

Ask about the staff-retention rate and the ratio of staff to patients. If there are only a few members who have been on the staff for any length of time, that may be a sign of trouble at the facility. If a facility cannot retain its staff, it may mean that the health-care workers are overworked and underpaid, or it may signal a more serious problem with the quality of care.

Look for staff members who bond with the patients and take a personal interest in them as they care for them over a period of time. Remember, the more staff per patient, the higher the quality of care you can expect.

3. *Are other services available beyond nursing care?* Your loved one may be in need of physical, occupational, speech, or respiratory therapy. Find out if the facility provides these. As in the case of Miss Lillian, such treatment may enable the patient to regain independence and leave the home.

Ask about opportunities for recreation. Some homes have movie nights and holiday celebrations; they throw birthday parties for their residents. Others welcome children's choirs and other groups from neighborhood schools and religious institutions to entertain. Some facilities offer pet therapy (during which residents can cuddle animals) and adopt-a-grandparent programs (through which residents can play with young children).

I was in Arizona recently working on an immunization program. One of the places I visited was a nursing home where the health department held weekly clinics to immunize the children of the community. The residents in the home had great fun entertaining the small children who came for their shots.

Inquire if nonambulatory patients are taken out for fresh air and sunshine daily, weather permitting. Some nursing homes even provide grooming facilities such as beauty parlors or barbershops.

Recreational therapy can include activities such as arts and crafts, sing-alongs, cooking classes, card games, and exercise classes. "Even bedridden and dementia patients should be included in activities," Cody explains. "No matter how advanced an individual's illness may be, stimulation through friendly conversation or touch therapy may be the key to his or her well-being." Some nursing homes have vans that transport patients to community events and entertainment.

You might also want to find out about religious activities. Confinement to a nursing home should not restrict one's right to participate in one's religion. Are worship services offered on site or is transportation available to nearby religious institutions? Are these services nondenominational, interdenominational, or otherwise appropriate for your loved one? Are there opportunities for private devotion? How often do clergy visit? Some nursing homes in our region of Georgia have clergy on staff. They give support and spiritual guidance to residents and their families.

But whatever the activities available, according to Ms. Cody, "You should not see residents unattended in hallways, sitting slumped over in their chairs."

4. *How good is the food?* You will want to know if a registered dietitian is working for the institution, especially if your loved one requires a specialized diet. Observe lunch service at the facility and ask yourself the following questions:

- Is the food delivered hot to the dining room and patients' rooms, or are the trays left out in the hallway for an hour before the staff can get to them?
- Does the food look and smell appetizing?
- Are well-balanced, healthful meals provided?
- Do people seem to be enjoying their meals? Are trays of food left untouched (bearing in mind that this may have less to do with the quality of the food than it does with the patients' condition)?
- If patients have trouble feeding themselves, are staff members helping them?

- Can the facility accommodate patients who require intravenous or tube feeding?

Depending on your family member's condition, you might also inquire if residents may be taken out for a meal from time to time, and if you may bring in favorite foods, as a treat.

5. *Is there a social worker on staff?* Social workers are valuable members of any nursing-home staff. They help patients adjust to their new environment and they help caregivers adjust to their changing role. For example, they can assist residents in obtaining government services. They can help procure devices such as prostheses, walkers, wheelchairs, and special shoes. They provide counseling and may help to organize a "family council."

6. *Is there a family council?* Some nursing homes in our area have family councils. These are composed of patients' family members who meet with the facility's leadership and staff once a month or quarterly to discuss mutual concerns. Members may even provide support for one another. Some family councils encourage social activities such as potluck dinners before the meetings.

7. *What is the condition of the facility?* Observe if the rooms, floors, and walls are clean and free of clutter. Then look for the following:

- Is there an unpleasant or overly perfumed odor? According to Ms. Cody, a good home will not need to use highly scented disinfectants to mask odors, but will maintain a cleaning schedule frequent enough to eliminate odors.
- Can patients bring familiar or comforting objects from home such as afghans, photographs, radios, television sets, or even

a favorite rocking chair? The presence of personal objects is a clue to whether patients are permitted to keep their identity and perhaps their dignity, or whether they must surrender these upon entering this particular facility.

- In rooms that accommodate more than one patient, do drapes or screens create a sense of privacy?
- Does each patient have a space for clothing and other personal belongings? Ask how often laundry is washed and how your loved one's clothing should be marked to prevent loss.
- Is a nurse call-button close to each patient's hand, especially those who are immobilized?
- Are bathrooms and shower rooms properly maintained? Are they private? Are they outfitted with rails, wide doors, or other devices that would aid the handicapped? Are there nurse call-buttons in the bathroom?

8. *What is the emotional climate at the home?* Look at the faces of the patients and the staff. Are they smiling? Do they seem sad or angry? Is the staff receptive and helpful? Are they supportive of one another? You might want to ask residents and visiting family members what they think of the home.

My friend who operates several nursing homes says that one of the best ways to judge a home is to just stand and watch how the staff relates to the residents. Do they speak to the residents as they walk by, smile at them, give them small reassurances—or, in his words, "Is there casual interaction?"

Now gauge your own response to being there. Do you feel relaxed or does the place make you uneasy? Your intuition and gut response are important.

9. *Can you work out the practical details?* Although an ideal facility may be available at some distance from your home, a less

than perfect one may prove to be more realistic if it is right around the block. Ask yourself how often you intend to visit and how important the facility's location is to you and other family members and friends. If you choose the more distant home, ask if there are telephones in the rooms for easy communication. If you choose the closer one, be sure that your frequent visits compensate for any negative attributes you have observed.

Find out about financial arrangements:

- Will you be able to afford the monthly payments?
- Does the facility accept benefits such as Medicaid as payment in full? Will Medicare cover nursing-home placement based on your family member's illness? (Medicare does not cover custodial or intermediate care and may not even cover skilled nursing care.)
- Will you be required to pay for prescriptions, diapers, or nutritional supplements? These can be costly. Are there other hidden expenses such as a charge for laundry, haircuts, or other personal grooming?
- Must you place a deposit to reserve a room? Is it refundable? What is the refund policy in general?
- Is it possible for patients to try the home for thirty days before making a more permanent commitment?

The more answers you have to your questions, the more secure you will feel in your decision to place your loved one in an institution.

REASSURANCE FROM THE PROFESSIONALS

Although family members are often reluctant to rely on nursing homes, many professionals in our CARE-NET survey expressed the hope that they might do so if the need arose. One nursing-home administrator said, "Family caregivers should understand that they don't need to feel guilty. Sometimes the best place for the patient is a professional setting." And another said, "Family members need to recognize that they can't do it all. They don't have the resources to give the patient proper care all the time. They need education as to what their normal limitations are. They shouldn't have to provide skilled care in their homes."

A registered nurse offered a compassionate view:

> Family members feel bad when they can't care for their loved one. They feel guilty. They need someone to tell them that they did a good job, to give them emotional support. I remind them that they have done an impossible thing. Here we get relief after eight hours, but at home they did not. I try to help their self-esteem. I tell them that if they had continued, then there would be two sick people.

And a nursing-home chaplain added, "My best experiences entail helping family members understand that this is the best thing for their loved ones; they aren't deserting them." Surely the nursing-home decision is a difficult one, but sometimes it is necessary.

A SENSE OF LOSS

Once the decision has been reached, many family caregivers face the future with some relief. Like Sissy Bowen, they begin to appreciate that they will get their lives, their homes, their freedom back. But they may also experience an intense feeling of loss. Family caregivers may believe they have lost their role, their importance, their familiar routines. Again, Sissy anticipated this emotion and described it eloquently in her letter to me shortly before she institutionalized her grandmother:

> For all these years, my entire life has revolved around caring for an Alzheimer's patient whom I love deeply. The separation and losses taking place are enormous, real, and heart-wrenching, and to think that any human being could withstand this transition without a lot of pain and anxiety is to have little understanding of humanity. . . .
>
> It does no good to deny myself the grief that anyone would feel in my shoes. I owe it to myself to allow these feelings to surface, so that I might really feel them, explore them, and understand them.

Then, only a few weeks later, Sissy described her actual reactions after taking her grandmother to the home. She published these observations in a column she writes as the editor of the Middle Flint Area Alzheimer's Support Group newsletter, *Caregiver's Companion*:

> I took Grandma to the nursing home this week. From the time I got the call, on Monday, until now, I think I've been in

shock. There are so many things in life that you just can't prepare for. I think this is one of those for me. There's no need to tell any of you how painful it was, to actually do the deed. You all can relate. What I do want to tell you is about how utterly lost I feel . . . just trying to live my life again.

It all started when I got the call. The lady from the nursing home said, "Can you bring her in tomorrow?"

"You see, Tuesday is the only weekday I have had a sitter in four years. So, with two appointments already on that day," I began to explain to the lady. . . . She had to interrupt me to tell me that after Tuesday, I wouldn't need a sitter anymore. I never prepared for that feeling.

Tuesday night was the first night in four and a half years that I slept in the house alone. With every bump, I'd rise to check on her. I still do . . . and probably will for a while. I woke up late, about nine-fifteen, Wednesday morning. Immediately I jumped up to see if she was OK. She wasn't there.

I've put the knobs back on the stove, but I keep opening the drawers to get them. I still look on top of the refrigerator for the sugar bowl, even though I put it back on the counter. I've had friends over . . . a rather unusual treat, and I still find myself lowering my voice so as not to bother her.

Although I know their intentions are good, I'm a little tired of people telling me, "You know, putting her in the nursing home was the best thing you could have done." I KNOW THAT! That's like telling me I should quit smoking . . . a bit rhetorical I think.

I see that I must take time, just for me, to nurture all that I am feeling and thinking and wanting and needing, so that I can better prepare for life without her.

Sissy experienced loss, but for her there was also the hope that she could find herself once more. Moreover, she now has the freedom and the desire to help others who are in the same demanding situation.

FINDING A BALANCE

Sometimes when loved ones move into a nursing home, family members and friends, for various reasons, stay away. This can be detrimental to the patient. As a nurse's aide in the CARE-NET study said:

> Family members play an important role. Even a confused resident knows when family is there. Some family members don't realize that. They think it doesn't matter if they visit. But it takes all of us working together. When a family member doesn't visit or bring something when the resident needs it, it can cause problems.

Other professionals have pointed out that the nursing home serves the resident's physical and medical needs whereas the family serves the emotional needs. Both are vital for total well-being. One woman in our CARE-NET study found a way to balance her need for respite with her guilt and her mother's need for care and attention. Here is how Trudy arranges her time:

> During the week, I visit my mother two to three times. I stay approximately one to two hours. On weekends, I visit three to five hours. During the week, I clean my mother's room. I pick up her laundry, give her the family news, read her mail, clean her dentures, and watch the news with her.

Mother likes Wendy's hamburgers, so I bring her one every Sunday. We go outside to the picnic area and eat. Then I take Mother for a ride to look at all the flowers. I encourage Mother to stay up because she always wants to go back to her room. When we do go back, we do personal grooming.

My mother looks forward to my visits. She always thanks me and is very grateful. It also lifts her spirits.

I feel closer to my mother now that I can go out and visit her. I feel good about the situation—more like a daughter. My worst experience was when Mother lived with me. I worked and would come home to people all over my house. I never had time to be alone. Sometimes I would speak sharply to Mother, but I don't get angry like I used to. I now have more control of the situation so I feel less resentment. I have more patience.

In the nursing home, I believe the family and caregiver should provide the person being cared for with emotional support and make sure quality care is being delivered. The professional should do the actual physical caring.

Trudy found a way to make institutionalization work for her and her mother. Perhaps, if the need arises, you will be able to make it work for you and your loved one, too.

11.

*F*INDING
FULFILLMENT

Throughout this book, I have described the many difficulties that family caregivers face: their fears, frustrations, and dilemmas. This is only natural. Guides such as this one deal mostly with problems and their solutions. But I don't want to leave you with the impression that caregiving is an onerous task with few rewards, for that would certainly be untrue.

Many participants in our CARE-NET study said that despite its difficulty, caregiving also fostered pleasure, love, personal growth, family closeness, and fulfillment. Some individuals were even able to reach beyond themselves and their own situations to help others in need. I find their stories inspiring and hope that you will draw strength and nourishment from them, too.

CAREGIVING CHANGES LIVES—FOR THE GOOD

"My attitudes and values have changed," said Margie. "I'm more of a human being—sensitive and caring. I've done a 180-degree change."

Margie's comments are typical of those of many lay caregivers in our study. When asked how caregiving had altered their lives, many said it changed them for the better. Most often they noted that it taught them to be more patient. But they grew in other ways, as well.

Here's how some caregivers found the experience improved their lives. I hope you identify with them and find their words as heartening as I did:

- "I feel once you know people and their problems, you can understand their needs. You are more sympathetic to those needs. I have learned to listen more to people. I do not believe people who are truly sick fake their problem."
- "I gained coping skills and learned self-preservation."
- "I wonder if I'm the same person I used to be. I feel I am more compassionate, more sensitive, more aware. I have learned that people want to maintain their dignity regardless of the problem they are having, whether it's physical or mental. . . . I think I have more of a sense of humor and am able to weed out trivial things."
- "I have more understanding . . . more empathy and sympathy for older people in general."
- "I think I've gotten much stronger. I strengthened my values. Caregiving has definitely enhanced my life. My family is

proud of my strength, my ability to communicate, and my humor."

- "Caregiving has taught me responsibility at an early age. I learned financial management. . . . It has made me appreciate what I have and appreciate the ability to reach out and help others. It has even taught my children to be more caring, to respect others, and to accept responsibility."
- "I'm no longer scared or depressed by mentally impaired people."
- "Caregiving has improved both my attitudes and my values. I am not bitter, and in the long run the experience has made me a better person. . . . It has improved my relationships with others. The relationships with my sisters are better because they have more respect for me. Caregiving has made me more mature."
- "The daily reality has caused me to be very grateful for the little things that improve in life."
- "There is more understanding about yourself. There is personal fulfillment. It is good to know you are able to take care of another person with a need. Caregiving has changed my life quite a bit. It made me see how blessed I am by not needing care. It taught me patience—that I'm not the only one in need, that others have needs, that they are not to be shut in a corner."
- "My whole concept of life and living has changed. I have a new respect for the process. Those being cared for need space, independence, and to be treated with respect and dignity."

These comments are a testament to the human spirit.

ADVOCACY

Margie felt that she had become a better person. She, along with several other caregivers in our study, also learned to take charge and advocate for her loved one. "Prior to the birth of my disabled son," she said, "I used to be quiet, shy, and polite. Now I'm an advocate—a fighter for the rights of all people, but especially the disabled. I know how laws and legislation work and don't work. And I know that some service providers do not provide services!"

When asked what advice she would give other lay caregivers, Margie said, "Empowerment: become a professional regarding your situation. Educate yourself: find out what is available in your community. Become active: advocate for your and your loved one's rights. Network with other caregivers. Give yourself dignity." Clearly, these are steps she has taken.

Helen talked about "making a difference and making the public aware of needs. . . . I see so much that needs to be done and isn't. It's frustrating. We need some priorities, and when those are not intact, it affects me in a negative way, and I want to fight hard."

And Eddie saw a need in his community and helped fill it. "Caregiving makes me very sympathetic to these people and gives me two types of feelings: one, being appreciative of what I've been blessed with; and two, that I'm able to help someone else." As a result, he built a group home for his mentally disabled adult stepson. "I was instrumental in establishing the home he lives in now," Eddie said. "I got help from two lawyers and politicians. We got a grant for $146,000 and built the home." Eddie's stepson resides there now with three other clients and nine employees.

Another caregiver who became involved in his community is Walter. Monday through Friday he spends time at the American Cancer Society's office, preparing informational packets for others. He attends two support meetings a month and serves on the board of directors. Recently he was asked to share his experiences as a caregiver during a seminar at his church. "The Cancer Society is my life's blood," he said. "It's what has made me able to cope with my situation. . . . My support comes from the other members of the group, and I hope I'm a support for them."

SATISFACTION

For many participants, caregiving sparked a sense of personal satisfaction in being able to help a friend or loved one. Beth said, "The best experiences are in the morning when we get Father up, dressed, groomed, and then have coffee. The rewards are small. I enjoy finding things that Dad will eat, and then [watching as] he eats it all. I enjoy seeing him comfortable."

Rose, who is caring for an unrelated mentally retarded, emotionally volatile older woman, said, "I cook for her, wash, take care of finances, mending, and doctor visits. She can keep her own room, but I clean behind her. My caregiving is voluntary, and I never regret it. I didn't like the way the state was taking care of Eleanore, so I brought her over to my home and family. . . . I have great satisfaction in watching her grow into a sound person."

Lynette, a mother caring for her disabled child, took great pleasure in her daughter's achievements. "Sarah is PROUD when she does something. It's rewarding to see her make an accomplishment—when she wants to do something and does it. When she hits the ball [while playing T-ball], it's wonderful."

Imagine the delight Charlene took when the person she was caring for—an unrelated older woman requiring supervision—improved. "When Wilma came to my house, she was in poor health, she disliked people, and she talked very little. Now she is very talkative, she has learned to care for herself, and she has learned the ABCs and how to write her name. She likes to be with people, and she's happier. . . . Our best experience was our first Christmas together. Wilma began to communicate. She expressed happiness at being part of a family. She had never experienced Christmas with gifts and family before."

And Babs, a young woman who provides care for three disabled relatives, said, "If I were not here, they would all be neglected and unhappy. I feel I make a difference in their lives. I don't get frustrated. This gives me something to do. It makes me feel good to do something for my people. It helped me to better understand the retarded and the handicapped. What I'm doing has improved my life and changed my attitude."

CAREGIVING STRENGTHENS FAMILIES AND PROMOTES LOVE

In Chapter 6, I covered the ways that caregiving can tear families apart. But many participants in our CARE-NET study also found that it strengthened bonds and brought their families closer.

For many, caregiving was an expression of love and devotion. As one caregiver put it, "She is my mother; she is my responsibility; she is my blessing. It is a privilege to do the care." Another said, "My son is a joy, not a burden." A third commented, "I am able to give back some of the love I had received from my father." And John, explaining why he visits his wife at the nursing home three to four times a week, said, "I've been told I go too much. I can't go any less. I love the lady too much."

Several other caregivers felt that their activities had strengthened their families. Lynette explained: "A friend said, 'I just would not want a handicapped child,' but I feel blessed to have the opportunity to do so. Sarah has brought the family closer." Another mother caring for a brain-damaged adult daughter said, "Our relationship has improved; as years go by, the closer I become to her. I am grateful for the years we have had so far." And a wife said of her husband, "The more I do, the closer we get. Caregiving has improved our relationship."

MOVING BEYOND

Fueled by the love they feel for their family members, the pain they've had to endure, and the desire to work toward the greater good, certain remarkable individuals have had the energy and internal resources to create programs that help other caregivers. One such person is Sissy Bowen, who co-founded the Alzheimer's support group in Americus, Georgia, and who is now helping to administer a state grant to increase services to people with Alzheimer's and their caregivers. Another is Suzanne Mintz, the wife of a man with multiple sclerosis. As I mentioned earlier, she is the co-founder of the National Family Caregivers Association.

Jerry Wise, whom you met in Chapter 5, is another of those who stand out in my mind. He was a childhood playmate of our son Jack, and the pain he has suffered has touched me deeply. Jerry shared his struggle and his triumphs with us at the Fourth Annual Conference of the Rosalynn Carter Institute:

> As a result [of our son's death], I'm here to tell you that life goes on.
>
> Realizing the helplessness and loneliness that we felt, God implanted in me an idea that I have let grow. About a year and a half ago, I started a grief support group here in Americus. I'm not a professional, but I've had some experiences. We meet every Monday night, and it's an informal opportunity for those who are going through the grief process to share.
>
> Our grief started at eighteen months of age for this young child. That's when it started and it's still going on. It's very deep; it's very personal.
>
> But in the group, we meet informally and share with one another. We hold on to one another. We cry with one another. We laugh with one another. And life goes on.
>
> There have been temptations to let life stop. But life goes on. And I'm here to tell you that there are people out there who are willing to be a supporting arm for those who are grieving, those who need help.
>
> Learn, take advantage of those opportunities, from those who are suffering beside you.

Through his tragic experience, Jerry has been able to help bring consolation to others in our community who grieve.

I have come across many caregivers who have been able to reach beyond themselves and their own problems to help others in similar situations. I would like to share with you one more remarkable story:

Rosemarie Mitchell is the mother of a severely disabled son. Teddy was a normal, attractive child until, at the age of six, he contracted a rare disease from a pet crow that left him brain-damaged. He is an adult now. His distorted, immobile body has to be moved with a lift from wheelchair to bed. He feeds through a tube; he does not talk. No one can tell whether he is aware of what goes on around him—no one except his mother! He requires, in her words, "twenty-four-hour watchful eyes. My typical day includes morning coffee with the spouse, and then [I] start with the bath and health care of my son. Most things can be accomplished if planned—shopping, other activities—but spontaneous things are difficult."

Through the years Rosemarie has encountered all the problems and hardships, both emotional and otherwise, that come with caregiving. And yet she has not let them defeat her. Several years after Teddy's illness, she went to school and became a licensed practical nurse (LPN) and an emergency medical technician (EMT). "My son gave me a career," she said. The new skills also helped her take better care of her son.

And amazingly, she and her husband, Ted, have never had anyone else care for Teddy. They schedule their work and other activities so that one is always home.

Rosemarie wants Teddy to have the experiences that well people have, so she takes him everywhere with her—in a specially designed van with a lift installed to pick him up in his wheelchair and put him into the van. The family has traveled to many places, including Hawaii and England. When interviewed for our CARE-NET survey, the family had just returned from a weekend at the beach. And when her other son joined the church, Rosemarie even took Teddy and had him baptized.

Rosemarie has been sustained, in great part, by her humor. She keeps anyone around her laughing. But she can also be very angry at the injustices suffered by those who are disabled: the lack of services, the need for respite, the lack of education that "would let children and adults know that there are many handicapped people and that they have many different disabilities . . . and that handicapped people are people with feelings and needs just as they have."

"I was in a bookstore with Teddy," she explained recently, "when a lady and her children entered the store. The three-year-old looked at Teddy and asked her mother, 'What's wrong with him?' pointing at my son. The mother just looked at me with horror, not knowing what to say. I then told the child, 'Teddy is handicapped.' The child asked no further questions and went on her merry way with just that simple explanation. The mother then thanked me for handling the situation."

Rosemarie has become an advocate for the disabled. She has even bungee-jumped for the cause—plunging from a basket 180 feet above the ground to help raise money for equipment for another disabled person in our community!

In a speech to the Governor's Council on Developmental Disabilities, she compared caregiving to bungee-jumping. "You have to experience it to know what it's like," she said. "The bungee jump lasts only a few seconds. What we go through as caregivers is going to last a lifetime for many of us, and until you have gone through the experience that we have, you can only guess what we go through every single day of our lives."

Yes, Rosemarie is an advocate, but she is much more.

Whether helping to raise money for another disabled person, building a wheelchair ramp for one who lives alone, or working on a Habitat for Humanity house for a poor family, she is always trying to help others. She recently told me about a new program she is involved in, called Parent to Parent. Members are parents of disabled people who try to help other parents. She had just traveled to a distant city to give practical advice and moral support to another mother with a severely disabled son.

"Because of me," she said, "they are going to get him a communications board. He is locked inside that body, almost like Teddy, but he can grip things; his fingers work a little. I believe he can communicate."

Rosemarie has spent almost thirty years as a caregiver. And when asked in our CARE-NET survey how caregiving had changed her life, she said, "It has improved my life. I am thankful for the years I have had with my son. My attitude is to value life and cherish the joy of living."

That's good advice for all of us.

Appendix A

LOOKING
TOWARD THE
FUTURE

After assessing the needs of informal and formal caregivers in our sixteen-county region of southwest Georgia, the research team conducting the CARE-NET study formulated policy and program recommendations for our community. I present them here, in the hope that communities around the country will also find them helpful. In some cases, I have generalized them to make them applicable to all situations, and I have limited the recommendations to those affecting family caregivers, since that is the focus of this book.

(A copy of the highlights of the study is available free of charge. If you'd like information on how to obtain the full report, which also covers the experiences and needs of formal caregivers, please write to the Rosalynn Carter Institute, Georgia Southwestern College, 800 Wheatley Street, Americus, GA 31709.)

POLICY AND PROGRAM
RECOMMENDATIONS

1. *Find ways for formal caregivers to spend more time with care receivers and informal caregivers.* Formal caregivers and agencies never think they have enough staff to serve their clients or patients properly. And recent cuts in state budgets coupled with increased administrative duties and paperwork have resulted in even fewer face-to-face interactions among them.

We recommend that more time be sought for professionals to spend with those receiving care and the family caregivers. The customary approach is to seek funds to hire more staff. An alternative would be to relieve professionals of some unnecessary paperwork, which would allow more time with clients. This change will require top-level decisions regarding priorities by agency administration and perhaps legislative bodies.

Volunteers and students might improve the situation in the meantime, and even after a policy change has been made.

2. *Understand the qualities of a caregiver.* All caregivers, formal and informal, share certain characteristics, attitudes, and orientations. We need to pay more attention to their common qualities rather than drawing rigid distinctions between professional and lay caregivers.

A caregiver, in general, is one who provides assistance to a person to help him/her feel better about, cope with, or cure a physical or mental health problem. Financial remuneration for the assistance, although sometimes necessary to the health-care provider, is not the prime motivation of the true care*giver.* Rather, his or her desire to help a loved one with a critical health problem is a defining quality.

Caregiving is simultaneously rewarding and burdensome. Helping others enhances one's own self-concept. Caregivers themselves require assistance, support, and recognition, and are susceptible to burnout if they lack the requisite skills, fail to receive help from others, or do not understand the scope of their task.

3. *Increase public and professional awareness of informal caregivers.* The majority of informal caregivers in our study were providing care for elderly individuals. Obviously, many people who are not considered elderly have chronic health problems and require care. It is important to recognize that people of all ages with varying levels of impairment at various times in their lives need the assistance of caregivers.

Some professional health-care providers fail to recognize the vital role of informal caregivers. These individuals, once the importance of their role is recognized, could be helped to better perform their duties as caregivers. Additionally, health-care professionals should realize that caregivers themselves often suffer—both emotionally and physically—because of their caregiving burden, and that they also require advice, assistance, and support. It is frustrating and depersonalizing to be ignored when you are providing the bulk of personal care, sometimes on a twenty-four-hour basis.

It is no wonder that some people seem reluctant to define themselves as caregivers. Perhaps they are concerned that the role will be too demanding or unappreciated, or that it will dramatically interfere with other aspects of their lives. These individuals require reassurance, commendation, and information about sources of assistance and support in their new role.

4. *Encourage academic institutions to assist caregivers.* Academic institutions could offer continuing education opportunities on

topics related to caregiving for family caregivers in their communities. They could add caregiving courses or at least add discussion of the topic to curricula, especially in the disciplines of nursing, psychology, counseling, social work, medicine, and education. They could also provide common ground for collaboration between formal and informal caregivers and offer caregiver assistance programs.

5. *Reexamine the role of religious institutions in providing concrete assistance to caregivers.* Most of the informal caregivers in our study felt that religious institutions were not providing adequate concrete assistance. Local congregations and ministerial associations should be encouraged to make decisions as to the appropriateness and importance of caregiving assistance, including help for their own members and for caregivers in the community at large.

6. *Socialize men for broader caregiving roles and responsibilities.* As with many other surveys, our CARE-NET study found that women do most of the hands-on caregiving. Men who describe themselves as family caregivers often do more of the financial and coordinating tasks, rather than provide direct care. This inequity will probably take years to change, but communities and organizations can take some steps to begin the process. They can promote seminars, discussion groups, articles, and forums that call attention to and deal with gender issues in caregiving.

As more and more people become involved in these programs, the gender issue should, over a period of time, begin to be less prominent. Research by psychologists Lenard Kaye and Jeffrey Applegate with 150 men who cared for ailing parents or spouses sixty hours a week found that when placed in the caregiving situation, men can be as supportive, loving, and competent as women.

7. *Support efforts to include informal caregivers in the "caregiving team."* Our CARE-NET study documented a lack of communication between formal and informal caregivers and distinct differences in the two groups' perceptions of adequacy of services provided by professionals. Informal caregivers' involvement as legitimate members of the cooperative treatment team should be emphasized in academic courses and during field experiences for students in professional training programs and by agency councils, boards, or other governing bodies.

Some professionals and family members may find it difficult to change their views on caregiving. Many professionals have been educated to focus on a dependent, powerless, and seriously ill "patient." They will need to develop a relationship with the informal caregiver as well, a basically healthy individual who has divergent insights, unique needs, and differing levels of status and power. On the other hand, family members and other informal caregivers may find it difficult to take more responsibility for providing care and to abandon stereotypic views of professional caregivers. Nevertheless, the ideal is a partnership in which formal and informal caregivers draw on one another's particular strengths.

8. *Provide training for informal caregivers.* Informal caregivers in our study indicated a need for more educational experiences to help them with their caregiving. A generic training program administered by local public or private agencies could focus on basic knowledge and skills needed by all caregivers. Such training should be carried out in relatively small groups of fifteen to twenty individuals each. In addition to providing knowledge and skills, such programs could also encourage the formation of

peer support groups and increase opportunities for communication and collaboration between formal and informal caregivers. Communities could also sponsor seminars and workshops on specific caregiving concerns.

9. *Create specific programs to help family caregivers.* Innovative programs designed specifically to help informal caregivers have been developed in Pennsylvania (Family Caregiver Support Program) and Oregon (Good Samaritan Education and Family Support Service). The program in Pennsylvania, for example, helps families who want to care for an older relative in their home. Some of the services offered are: assessment of caregiver needs; counseling in coping skills; respite care; training in caregiving skills; counseling regarding benefits of local, state, and federal programs; and one-time grants for home adaptations.

10. *Establish community resource consultants for family caregivers.* Community resource consultants are individuals who link family caregivers with resources within the community. They also assist family caregivers in identifying options available to them, provide emotional support and information, and serve as advocates when necessary. These consultants, though similar to "case managers," would not be connected to any one specific service agency. (Ombudsmen programs already in existence usually address specific complaints.) Funding for such consultants could come from federal, state, or local funds or from private foundations.

11. *Create resource centers.* Communities could establish caregiver information resource centers within libraries or other already existing institutions to serve as clearinghouses for information about caregiving. Caregivers could visit the center or

request that information in the form of books, pamphlets, video or audio tapes, and journals be sent to their homes.

12. *Establish short-term, limited financial grants to family caregivers.* Some of caregivers' financial needs directly related to caregiving responsibilities are often not addressed by public funding sources or private insurance policies. Short-term, limited-amount grants available to family caregivers could help them with special equipment or supplies, in-home nursing care, respite care, or other needs on an emergency basis. Or these funds could be made available for situations in which the financial needs of the family "fall between the cracks" of eligibility requirements of major funding programs. Funds for such a program could come from government sources or they could be raised from foundations or local organizations such as civic clubs or churches.

13. *Increase public awareness and media attention regarding the rewards and burdens of caregiving.* Informal caregivers in the CARE-NET study felt they received little recognition in the media. We recommend an ongoing public awareness campaign including, but not limited to, feature articles in local and national newspapers, regional television and radio talk show segments, public service announcements, national news magazine shows, and speakers' bureaus for local and statewide civic clubs and organizations.

Such a campaign would accomplish two objectives: it would provide recognition and reinforcement for caregivers, and it would increase the likelihood of public support for more programs and services for them.

Appendix B

HELPFUL ORGANIZATIONS AND RESOURCES

SELF-HELP CLEARINGHOUSES

The American Self-Help
  Clearinghouse
St. Clare's-Riverside Medical
  Center
25 Pocono Rd.
Denville, NJ 07834
(201) 625-7101

California Self-Help Center
405 Hilgard Ave.
Los Angeles, CA 90024
If in California (800) 222-5465
Out of state (310) 825-1799

National Mental Health
  Consumer's Self-Help
  Clearinghouse*
311 S. Juniper St., Room 1000
Philadelphia, PA 19107
(215) 735-6082
(800) 553-4539

The National Self-Help
  Clearinghouse
City University of New York
Room 620
25 West 43rd St.
New York, NY 10036
(212) 642-2944

*Member of the National Quality Caregiving Coalition (NQCC) of the Rosalynn
Carter Institute.

Self-Help Center
1600 Dodge Ave. Suite S-122
Evanston, IL 60201
If in Illinois (800) 322-MASH
Out of state (708) 328-0471

INFORMATION CLEARINGHOUSES
(Alphabetical by condition)

Brookdale Center for **Aging**
(800) 648-COPE
National information clearinghouse for adult day-care referrals.

Eldercare Locator (**Aging**)
(800) 677-1116
A public service, operating in conjunction with the U.S. Administration on Aging, that provides referrals to local community agencies for home care, respite services, adult day care, senior centers, legal assistance, home-delivered meals, and transportation.

Centers for Disease Control
  National **AIDS** Clearinghouse
P.O. Box 6003
Rockville, MD 20850
(800) 458-5231

National Clearinghouse for
  Alcohol and Drug
  Information
P.O. Box 2345
Rockville, MD 20852
(301) 468-2600
(800) 729-6686

National **Arthritis,**
  Musculoskeletal, and **Skin**
  Diseases
Information Clearinghouse
(301) 495-4484

Cancerfax
(301) 402-5874 for instructions
  and codes
This service allows access to the National Cancer Institute's Physician's Data Query system via fax machine. Information available for professionals and also for patients and family members.

Cancer Information Service
Office of Cancer
Communications
National Cancer Institute/
National Institutes of Health
Building 31, 10A24
9000 Rockville Pike
Bethesda, MD 20892

National Alliance of Breast
Cancer Organizations
(NABCO)
1180 Ave. of the Americas, 2nd
Floor
New York, NY 10036
(212) 719-0154
Clearinghouse for breast cancer informa-
tion.

National Information Center on
Deafness
Gallaudet University
800 Florida Ave. NE
Washington, DC 20002
(202) 651-5051

National Information
Clearinghouse for Infants with
Developmental Disabilities
and Life-Threatening
Conditions
University of South Carolina
School of Medicine, Dept. of
Pediatrics
Columbia, SC 29208

(800) 922-9234, ext. 201 (Voice
and TT)

National Diabetes Information
Clearinghouse
Box NDIC
9000 Rockville Pike
Bethesda, MD 20892
(301) 654-3327

National Digestive Diseases
Information Clearinghouse
Box NDDIC
9000 Rockville Pike
Bethesda, MD 20892
(301) 654-3810

Clearinghouse on Disability
Information
Office of Special Education and
Rehabilitative Services
U.S. Department of Education
Room 3132, Switzer Building
Washington, DC 20202-2524
(202) 205-8241
Ask for "The Pocket Guide to Federal
Help for Individuals with Disabilities."

National Information Center for
Children and Youth with
Disabilities
P.O. Box 1492
Washington, DC 20013
(800) 999-5599
(800) 695-0285

National **Health** Information
  Center
(800) 336-4797

National **Heart, Lung, Blood**
  Institute Information Center
(301) 251-1222
*For information on high blood pressure,
heart disease, cholesterol, smoking, lung
diseases, and blood diseases.*

National **Kidney and Urologic
Diseases** Information
Clearinghouse
P.O. Box NKUDIC
9000 Rockville Pike
Bethesda, MD 20892
(301) 654-4415

National Jewish **Lung** Line
  Information Service
(800) 222-LUNG

National Center for Education
  in **Maternal and Child** Health
  (Formerly, National
  Clearinghouse for Human
  Genetic Diseases)
(703) 524-7802

National **Maternal and Child**
  Health Clearinghouse
(202) 625-8410

National **Mental Health**
  Consumer Self-Help
  Clearinghouse
311 S. Juniper St., Suite 902
Philadelphia, PA
(800) 688-4226

National Organization for **Rare**
  Disorders
P.O. Box 8923
New Fairfield, CT 06812
(800) 999-NORD

National Center for **Substance**
  Abuse Prevention, Workplace
  Helpline
Department AL
P.O. Box 1909
Rockville, MD 20852
(800) 843-4971
*For information on creating a drug-free
workplace.*

HOTLINES
(Alphabetical by condition)

The CDC National **AIDS**
Hotline
(800) 342-AIDS

National **Autism** Hotline
(304) 525-8014

National **Burn** Victim
Foundation Hotline
(201) 676-7700

American **Cancer** Society
(800) ACS-2345

National **Cancer** Institute,
Cancer Information Service
(800) 4-CANCER

Chemocare (**Cancer**)
(800) 55-CHEMO
(908) 233-1103 in New Jersey
*National agency that matches cancer
patients with volunteers who have had a
similar diagnosis. Volunteers provide
emotional support on the phone or in
person, if possible.*

Cocaine Hotline
(800) COCAINE

National **Insurance** Consumer
Helpline
(800) 942-4242

Medicare Hotline
(800) 638-6833

American **Paralysis** Association
Spinal Cord Injury Hotline
(800) 526-3456

Center for **Substance Abuse**
Treatment, National Drug
Information Treatment and
Referral Hotline
(800) 662-HELP
(800) 66-AYUDA in Spanish

Second **Surgical** Opinion
Hotline (Medicare)
(800) 638-6833
*Will connect you with agencies in your
area which will refer three qualified doctors.*

Social Security Administration
Hotline
(800) 772-1213
(800) 325-0778 (TTD)

Suicide and Crisis Hotline
(800) 333-4444 (24-hour
service)

217

GENERAL ORGANIZATIONS
(Listed alphabetically)

Administration for Children and Families
ACF Aerospace Building, Suite 600
370 L'Enfant Promenade SW
Washington, DC 20447
(202) 401-9200

Adventures in Movement for the Handicapped
945 Danbury Rd.
Dayton, OH 45420
(513) 294-4611

American Association of Homes for the Aging (AAHA)
901 E Street NW, Suite 500
Washington, DC 20004
(202) 783-2242
Ask for the pamphlet "Choosing a Nursing Home: A Guide to Quality Care."

American Association of Pastoral Counselors*
9504-A Lee Highway
Fairfax, VA 22031
(703) 385-6967

American Association of Retired Persons (AARP)*
601 E Street NW
Washington, DC 20049

(800) 424-2277
Offers many free informational pamphlets, such as "The Caregiver Resource Kit" (D15267), "A Handbook About Care in the Home: Information on Home Care Services," "Nursing Home Life: A Guide for Residents and Families," "Medicare: What It Covers, What It Doesn't," "Miles Away and Still Caring: A Handbook for Long-Distance Caregivers."

American Disability Association
2121 8th Ave. N., Suite 1623
Birmingham, AL 35203
(205) 323-3030

American Hospital Association*
840 N. Lakeshore Dr.
Chicago, IL 60611
(312) 280-6495

American Medical Association*
515 N. State St.
Chicago, IL 60610
(312) 464-4818

American Nurses Association*
600 Maryland Ave. SW, Suite 100-West
Washington, DC 20024
(202) 554-4444

The Association for Persons
with Severe Handicaps
11201 Greenwood Ave. N
Seattle, WA 98113
(206) 361-8870

Care for Life
(312) 880-4630
*For individuals dependent on life-support
systems.*

Centers for Disease Control*
1600 Clifton Rd., Mailstop E-44
Atlanta, GA 30333
(404) 639-8276

City of Hope
1500 E. Duarte Rd.
Duarte, CA 91010
(818) 359-8111
*Treatment and research in catastrophic
diseases; referral services for cancer, leukemia, blood disorders, lung disease,
heart disease, diabetes, Alzheimer's disease, AIDS, etc.*

COMPEER, Inc.*
Monroe Square, Suite B-1
259 Monroe Ave.
Rochester, NY 14607
(716) 546-8280
*Matches volunteers with people needing
assistance.*

Concerned Relatives of Nursing
Home Patients
P.O. Box 18820
Cleveland Heights, OH 44118
(216) 321-0403

Emory University School of
Medicine*
Woodruff Memorial Building
P.O. Box AF
Atlanta, GA 30322
(404) 248-3688

The Family Caregiver Alliance
(formerly The Family Survival
Project)
425 Bush St., Suite 500
San Francisco, CA 94108
If in California (800) 445-8106
Out of state (415) 434-3388

Federation for Children with
Special Needs
95 Berkeley St., Suite 104
Boston, MA 02116
(800) 331-0688
(617) 482-2915

HEALTH Resource Center
One Dupont Circle, Suite 800
Washington, DC 20036
(800) 544-3284
*Information on all aspects of education
and training beyond high school for
people with disabilities.*

National Association of Area
  Agencies on Aging
1112 16th St. NW, Suite 100
Washington, DC 20036
(202) 296-8130

National Consortium on
  Interprofessional Education &
  Practice*
4418 Vale Circle
Madison, WI 53711

National Council on Aging
409 3rd St. SW, Suite 200
Washington, DC 20024
(202) 479-1200
(800) 424-9046
*The Directory of Adult Day Care in
America is order #2022.*

National Family Caregivers
  Association
9223 Longbranch Parkway
Silver Spring, MD 20901-3641
(301) 949-3638

National Federation of Interfaith
  Volunteer Caregivers, Inc.*
368 Broadway, Suite 103
P.O. Box 1939
Kingston, NY 12401
(914) 331-1358

The National Home Caring
  Council
67 Irving Place
New York, NY 10003
(212) 674-4990
*For information on appropriate in-home
services.*

National Institute of Child
  Health and Human
  Development
(301) 496-3454

National Institute on
  Community-Based Long-Term
  Care
(202) 479-6680

The National Organization for
  Rare Disorders
P.O. Box 8923
New Fairfield, CT 06812-1783
(203) 746-6518
(800) 999-NORD

Older Women's League
666 11th St. NW, Suite 700
Washington, DC 20001
(202) 783-6686
*Advocacy group for women caregivers
in their later years.*

Parents of Chronically Ill
  Children
1527 Maryland St.
Springfield, IL 62702
(217) 522-6810

Parents Helping Parents
535 Race St., Suite 120
San Jose, CA 95126
(408) 288-5010
Helps children with special needs receive care, services, and education. Education, support, and training for parents.

Parent to Parent Network
c/o Betsy Santelli
Beach Center on Families and
  Disabilities
University of Kansas, Institute
  for Lifespan Studies
3111 Haworth Hall
Lawrence, KS 66045
(913) 864-7606

Parent to Parent of Georgia, Inc.
2939 Flowers Road South, Suite
  131
Atlanta, GA 30341
(404) 451-5484
(800) 229-2038 in Georgia

The Rosalynn Carter Institute
  for Human Development
Georgia Southwestern College*
800 Wheatley St.
Americus, GA 31709-4693
(912) 928-1234

Siblings of Disabled Children
535 Race St., Suite 120
San Jose, CA 95126
(408) 288-5010

Sick Kids Need Involved People
  (SKIP)
(410) 647-0164
For children who are dependent on life-support systems.

The Well Spouse Foundation*
P.O. Box 28876
San Diego, CA 92198
(619) 673-9043

HOSPICE ORGANIZATIONS

Children's Hospice International
901 N. Washington St., Suite
  700
Alexandria, VA 22314
(703) 684-0330
(800) 242-4453

Hospice Association of America
519 C St. NE
Stanton Park
Washington, DC 20002
(202) 546-4759

Hospice Foundation*
1 Southeast Third Ave., Suite
    1220
Miami, FL 33131

National Hospice Organization
1901 N. Moore St., Suite 901
Arlington, VA 22209
(800) 658-8898

ORGANIZATIONS BY CONDITION

AGING

Administration on Aging
330 Independence Ave. SW
Washington, DC 20201

American Association for
    Geriatric Psychiatry
P.O. Box 376-A
Greenbelt, MD 20768
(301) 220-0952

American Association of Retired
    Persons (AARP)*
601 E Street NW
Washington, DC 20049
(800) 424-2277

American Society on Aging
(415) 882-2910

Association for Adult
    Development and Aging
c/o American Counseling
    Association
(703) 823-9800

Children of Aging Parents
(215) 945-6900

Gerontological Society of
    America
(202) 842-1275

National Council on the Aging
(800) 424-9046

National Institute of Mental
    Health, Aging Branch
(301) 443-1185

National Support Center for
    Families of the Aging
(215) 544-5933

AIDS

AIDS Clinical Trials Group
National Institutes of Health
6003 Executive Blvd., Room
  2A07
Bethesda, MD 20892
(301) 496-8210
Federal government program that coordinates testing of experimental drugs used in AIDS treatment.

American Foundation for AIDS
  Research (AmFAR)
5900 Wilshire Blvd.
Los Angeles, CA 90036
(213) 857-5900

Families Who Care
6475 Pacific Coast Highway,
  Suite 202
Long Beach, CA 90803-4296
(310) 498-6366
For information on how to start your own AIDS family support group.

HIV Information Exchange and
  Support Group
610 Greenwood
Glenview, IL 60025
(708) 724-3832
Support group and peer counseling based on adaptation of 12-step program.

Mothers of AIDS Patients
1811 Field Drive NE
Albuquerque, NM 87112
(619) 544-0430
Forty groups nationwide; provides support for families of AIDS patients.

National Minority AIDS Council
(202) 544-1076

Pediatric AIDS Foundation
1311 Colorado Ave.
Santa Monica, CA 90404
(310) 395-9051
Provides informational resources, free parent-education programs, emergency assistance grants, research into blocking transmission from pregnant mothers to newborns, and research grants and scholar awards.

Tennessee Department of
  Health, STD and HIV
  Program
312 8th Ave., North 13th Floor
Tennessee Tower
Nashville, TN 37247-4947
(615) 741-7500
(800) 525-2437 in Tennessee
  only
A notebook on living healthy with HIV is available to Tennessee residents only.

The U.S. Department of Health
and Human Services
Public Health Services
Centers for Disease Control
(404) 639-3311
(800) 368-1019

ALLERGY AND ASTHMA

American Allergy Association
P.O. Box 7273
Menlo Park, CA 94026
(415) 322-1663

Asthma and Allergy Foundation
of America
1125 15th St. NW, Suite 502
Washington, DC 20005
(202) 466-7643

National Allergy and Asthma
Network
3554 Chain Bridge Road, Suite
200
Fairfax, VA 22030-2709
(703) 385-4403
Support for parents and practical advice.

ALZHEIMER'S DISEASE

Alzheimer's Disease & Related
Disorders Association, Inc.*
919 N. Michigan Ave., Suite
1000
Chicago, IL 60611-1676
(800) 272-3900

AMPUTATION

American Amputee Foundation
P.O. Box 250218, Hillcrest
Station
Little Rock, AR 72225
(501) 666-2523

National Amputation Foundation
12–45 150th St.
Whitestone, NY 11357
(718) 767-0596

AMYOTROPIC LATERAL SCLEROSIS
(ALS, or Lou Gehrig's Disease)

ALS and Neuromuscular
Research Foundation
c/o California Pacific Medical
Center
2351 Clay St., Suite 416
San Francisco, CA 94115
(415) 923-3640

ALS Association
21021 Ventura Blvd.
Woodland Hills, CA 91364
(800) 782-4747
Information and referral service, support groups, counseling.

ARTHRITIS

The American Juvenile Arthritis
  Foundation
(800) 283-7800
(404) 872-7100

The Arthritis Foundation
1314 Spring St.
Atlanta, GA 30309
(800) 283-7800

AUTISM

Autism Network International
P.O. Box 1545
Lawrence, KS 66044

Autism Services Center
Prichard Building
605 9th St.
P.O. Box 507
Huntington, WV 25710-0507
(304) 525-8014

Autism Society of America
7910 Woodmont Ave., Suite 650
Bethesda, MD 20814
(800) 3AU-TISM

BIRTH DEFECTS

Association of Birth Defect
  Children
Orlando Executive Park
5400 Diplomat Circle, Suite 270
Orlando, FL 32810
(407) 859-2821

March of Dimes Birth Defects
  Foundation
1275 Mamaroneck Ave.
White Plains, NY 10605
(914) 428-7100

BLOOD DISORDERS

Aplastic Anemia Foundation of
  America
P.O. Box 22689
Baltimore, MD 21203
(800) 747-2820

Cooley's Anemia Foundation
105 E. 22nd St., Suite 911
New York, NY 10010
(212) 598-0911

National Rare Blood Club
164 Fifth Ave.
New York, NY 10010
(212) 889-4455
Organization for individuals with rare blood types.

See also listings under **Hemophilia, Leukemia, Sickle-Cell Anemia**

BURNS

American Burn Association
(800) 548-2876

National Burn Victim Foundation
(201) 676-7700

Phoenix Society for Burn
  Survivors
(215) 946-BURN

CANCER

American Brain Tumor
  Association
3725 N. Talman Ave.
Chicago, IL 60618
(312) 286-5571

American Cancer Society
1599 Clifton Road NE
Atlanta, GA 30329
(800) 227-2345

Breast Cancer Advisory Center
P.O. Box 224
Kensington, MD 20895

Cancer Care
(212) 221-3300

Candlelighters Childhood
  Cancer Foundation
(301) 657-8401
Educates and supports family members with children or adolescents with cancer.

DES Action, U.S.A.
(510) 465-4011
Education and support for women whose mothers took the synthetic hormone DES (diethylstilbestrol) during pregnancy.

Make Today Count
P.O. Box 6063
Kansas City, KS 66106-0063

National Bone Marrow
  Transplant Program
3433 Broadway St. NE, Suite
  400
Minneapolis, MN 55413
(800) MARROW-2
(612) 627-5800

National Children's Cancer
Society
1015 Locust St., Suite 1040
St. Louis, MO 63101-1323
(800) 532-6459
(314) 241-1600

National Coalition for Cancer
Survivorship
1010 Wayne Ave., Suite 300
Silver Spring, MD 20910
(301) 585-2616

Reach to Recovery
c/o American Cancer Society
1599 Clifton Rd. NE
Atlanta, GA 30329
(404) 320-3333
*Peer-visitor program for women who
have breast cancer.*

Skin Cancer Foundation
245 Fifth Ave., Suite 2402
New York, NY 10016
(212) 725-5176

US TOO
c/o American Foundation for
Urologic Diseases
300 W. Pratt St., Suite 401
Baltimore, MD 21201
(800) 242-2383
*Patient support groups for prostate can-
cer survivors.*

The Wellness Community,
National
2716 Ocean Park Blvd., Suite
1030
Santa Monica, CA 90405
(310) 314-2555
*Psychosocial support groups for cancer
patients and their families in fifteen cities.*

Y-ME National Organization for
Breast Cancer Information and
Support
18220 Harwood Ave.
Homewood, IL 60430
(800) 221-2141
(708) 799-8338

CEREBRAL PALSY

United Cerebral Palsy
Associations
(800) 872-5827

CHRONIC FATIGUE
SYNDROME/
EPSTEIN-BARR VIRUS
SYNDROME

CFIDS Association
(800) 442-3437

Chronic Fatigue Syndrome
Foundation
(800) 237-2407
(800) 597-4237

National Chronic Fatigue
Syndrome Association
(816) 931-4777

CYSTIC FIBROSIS

Cystic Fibrosis Foundation
6931 Arlington Road
Bethesda, MD 20814
(800) FIGHT-CF

DEAF-BLIND

American Association of the
Deaf-Blind
814 Thayer Ave., Room 300
Silver Spring, MD 20910
(301) 587-1788

Helen Keller National Center
for Deaf-Blind Youths and
Adults
111 Middle Neck Road
Sands Point, NY 11050
(516) 944-8900

DEVELOPMENTAL DISABILITIES

Administration on
Developmental Disabilities
200 Independence Ave. SW
Suite 349D—HHH Building
Washington, DC 20201
(202) 690-6590

National Center for Youth with
Disabilities
University of Minnesota
420 Delaware St. SE
P.O. Box 721
Minneapolis, MN 55455-0392
(800) 333-6293

DIABETES

American Diabetes Association
P.O. Box 25757
1660 Duke St.
Alexandria, VA 22314
(800) 828-8293

Juvenile Diabetes Foundation
International
432 Park Ave. South
New York, NY 10016-8013
(800) JDF-CURE

National Service Center
(800) 232-3472
(203) 549-1500

DIGESTIVE DISORDERS

Celiac Sprue Association/USA
P.O. Box 31700
Omaha, NB 68131-0700
(402) 558-0600

Crohn's and Colitis Foundation
of America
444 Park Ave. South, 11th Floor
New York, NY 10016-7343
(212) 685-3440
(800) 932-2423

North American Society for
Pediatric Gastroenterology
and Nutrition
Children's Hospital
1056 19th Ave.
Denver, CO 80218
(303) 861-6669

EATING DISORDERS

Anorexia Nervosa and Related
Eating Disorders
P.O. Box 5102
Eugene, OR 97405
(503) 344-1144

National Association of Anorexia
Nervosa and Associated
Disorders
P.O. Box 7
Highland Park, IL 60035
(708) 831-3438

EPILEPSY

Epilepsy Concern Service Group
1282 Wynnewood Drive
West Palm Beach, FL 33417
(407) 683-0044
*For information on how to start your
own peer support group.*

Epilepsy Foundation of America
4351 Garden City Drive
Landover, MD 20785
(800) EFA-1000
(301) 459-3700

GENETIC DISEASES
(General)

Alliance of Genetic Support
Groups
35 Wisconsin Circle, Suite 440
Chevy Chase, MD 20815
(202) 625-7853
(800) 336-GENE

Council of Regional Networks
for Genetic Services
Cornell University Medical
College
1300 York Ave., Genetics
Box 53
New York, NY 10021
(212) 746-3475

National Foundation for Jewish
Genetic Diseases
250 Park Ave., Suite 1000
New York, NY 10077
(212) 371-1030

National Tay-Sachs and Allied
Diseases Association
2001 Beacon St.
Brookline, MA 02146
(617) 277-4463

HEADACHE

National Headache Foundation
(312) 878-7715

HEAD INJURY AND COMA

Coma Recovery Association
377 Jerusalem Ave.
Hempstead, NY 11550
(516) 486-2847
Support for coma and head injury sur-
vivors and their families.

National Head Injury
Foundation
1776 Massachusetts Ave. NW,
Suite 100
Washington, DC 20036
(202) 296-6443
(800) 444-6443

HEARING IMPAIRMENT

Alexander Graham Bell
Association for the Deaf
3417 Volta Place NW
Washington, DC 20007
(202) 337-5220

National Association for the
Deaf
814 Thayer Ave.
Silver Spring, MD 20910
(301) 587-1788

Self-Help for Hard of Hearing
People
(301) 657-2248

HEART

American Heart Association,
National Center
7272 Greenville Ave.
Dallas, TX 75231
(214) 373-6300
(800) 242-8721

The Coronary Club, Inc.
9500 Euclid Ave.
Cleveland, OH 44106
(216) 444-3690

Heartmates Support Groups
P.O. Box 16202
Minneapolis, MN 55416
Written requests only.

International Bundle Branch
   Block Association
(310) 670-9132

Mended Hearts
c/o American Heart Association
7272 Greenville Ave.
Dallas, TX 75231
(214) 706-1442
*For persons who have heart disease, their
families and friends.*

National Heart, Lung and Blood
   Institute Information Center
7200 Wisconsin Ave.
P.O. Box 329
Bethesda, MD 20814
(301) 251-1222

HEMOPHILIA

National Hemophilia Foundation
(212) 219-8180

HYDROCEPHALUS

National Hydrocephalus
   Foundation
400 N. Michigan Ave., Suite
   1102
Chicago, IL 60611-4102
(312) 645-0701
(815) 467-6548

HYPERTENSION
(High blood pressure)

American Society of
   Hypertension
515 Madison Ave., Suite 2100
New York, NY 10022
(212) 644-0650

Citizens for Public Action on
   Blood Pressure and
   Cholesterol
7200 Wisconsin Ave., Suite 1002
Bethesda, MD 20814
(301) 907-7790

The National Hypertension
   Association
324 E. 30th St.
New York, NY 10016
(212) 889-3557

IMMUNE DEFICIENCY
DISEASES

Immune Deficiency Foundation
P.O. Box 586
Columbia, MD 21045
(410) 461-3127

INCONTINENCE

Help for Incontinent People
P.O. Box 544
Union, SC 92379
(803) 579-7900
(800) BLADDER

I Will Manage Self-Help Groups
Simon Foundation for
  Continence
P.O. Box 815
Wilmette, IL 60091
(708) 864-3913
(800) 23 SIMON
*Support for people with urinary or
bowel incontinence.*

KIDNEY DISEASE

American Association of Kidney
  Patients
111 S. Parker St., Suite 405
Tampa, FL 33606
(800) 749-2257

American Kidney Fund
6110 Executive Blvd. #1010
Rockville, MD 20852
(410) 381-3052

Kidney Transplant/Dialysis
  Association
(617) 267-3747

National Kidney Foundation
30 E. 33rd St., Suite 1100
New York, NY 10016
(212) 889-2210
(800) 622-9010

LEUKEMIA

Leukemia Society of America
600 Third Ave.
New York, NY 10016
(212) 573-8484
(800) 955-4LSA

National Leukemia Association
585 Stewart Ave., Suite 536
Garden City, NY 11530
(516) 222-1944

LIVER DISEASE

American Liver Foundation
(800) 223-0179

LUNG DISEASE

American Lung Association
1740 Broadway
New York, NY 10019-4374
(212) 315-8700
(800) LUNG-USA

Asbestos Victims of America
P.O. Box 559
Capitola, CA 95010
(408) 476-3646

Brown Lung Association
P.O. Box 7583
Greenville, SC 29610
(803) 269-8048

Care for Life
1018 Diversey Parkway
Chicago, IL 60614
(312) 883-1018
For individuals dependent on respirators.

Emphysema Anonymous
P.O. Box 3224
Seminole, FL 34642
(813) 391-9977

National Association for
Ventilator Dependent
Individuals
3601 Poplar St.
P.O. Box 3666
Erie, PA 16508
(814) 455-6171

National Jewish Center for
Immunology and Respiratory
Medicine
1400 Jackson St.
Denver, CO 80206
(800) 222-LUNG
Nonsectarian. Treatment, research, education in chronic respiratory diseases.

LUPUS ERYTHEMATOSUS

The American Lupus Society
3914 Del Amo Blvd., Suite 922
Torrance, CA 90503
(310) 542-8891

L.E. Support Club
8039 Nova Court
North Charleston, SC 92420
(803) 764-1769

The Lupus Foundation of
America
(800) 558-0121
(800) 800-4532

MENTAL HEALTH

American Academy of Child and
  Adolescent Psychiatry*
3615 Wisconsin Ave. NW
Washington, D.C. 20016
(202) 966-7300

American Association for
  Marriage and Family Therapy*
1100 17th St. NW, 10th Floor
Washington, D.C. 20036
(202) 452-0109

American Psychiatric
  Association*
1400 K Street NW
Washington, DC 20005
(202) 682-6000

American Psychological
  Association*
750 First St. NE
Washington, DC 20002-4242
(202) 336-5500

American Schizophrenia
  Association
900 N. Federal Highway, Suite
  330
Boca Raton, FL 33432
(407) 393-6167

Anxiety Disorders Association of
  America*
6000 Executive Blvd., Suite 513
Rockville, MD 20852
(301) 231-9350

Black Psychiatrists of America*
2730 Adeline St.
Oakland, CA 94607
(510) 465-1800

Depression and Related Affective
  Disorders Association
Johns Hopkins Hospital
Meyer 3-181
600 N. Wolfe St.
Baltimore, MD 21205
(410) 955-4647

Foundation for Depression and
  Manic Depression
7 E. 67th St.
New York, NY 10021
(212) 772-3400

National Alliance for the
  Mentally Ill*
2101 Wilson Blvd., Suite 302
Arlington, VA 22201
(800) 950-NAMI
(703) 524-7600

National Association of Private
  Psychiatric Hospitals*
1319 F St. NW, Suite 1000
Washington, DC 20004
(202) 393-6700

National Association of Social
  Workers*
750 First Street NE, Suite 700
Washington, DC 20002-4241
(202) 336-8200

National Council for
  Community Mental Health
  Centers*
12300 Twinbrook Parkway, Suite
  320
Rockville, MD 20852
(301) 984-6200

National Institute of Mental
  Health
U.S. Department of Health and
  Human Services
5600 Fishers Lane, Room 10-85
Rockville, MD 20857
(800) 421-4211

National Mental Health
  Association*
1021 Prince St.
Alexandria, VA 22314
(800) 969-NMHA
(703) 684-7722

Obsessive Compulsive
  Foundation
P.O. Box 9573
New Haven, CT 06535
(203) 772-0565

MENTAL RETARDATION AND DOWN SYNDROME

American Association on Mental
  Retardation*
1719 Kalorama Road NW
Washington, D.C. 20009
(202) 387-1968

The ARC (mentally disabled)
500 E. Border St., Suite 300
Arlington, TX 76010
(817) 261-6003

Association for Children with
  Down Syndrome
2616 Martin Ave.
Bellmore, NY 11710
(516) 221-4700

Center for Family Support
  (mentally disabled)
386 Park Ave. South
New York, NY 10016
(212) 481-1082

Council for Exceptional
Children
1920 Association Drive
Reston, VA 22091-1589
(703) 620-3660

National Down Syndrome
Society
666 Broadway
New York, NY 10012
(800) 221-4602

Parents of Down Syndrome
Children
11600 Nebel St.
Rockville, MD 20852
(301) 984-5792

MULTIPLE SCLEROSIS

Multiple Sclerosis Foundation
6350 N. Andrews Ave.
Fort Lauderdale, FL 33309
(305) 776-6805

National Multiple Sclerosis
Society
733 Third Ave.
New York, NY 10017
(212) 986-3240
(800) FIGHT-MS

MUSCULAR DYSTROPHY

Muscular Dystrophy Association
3300 E. Sunrise Drive
Tucson, AZ 85718
(602) 529-2000

NEUROLOGICAL DISORDERS

National Institute of
Neurological Disorders and
Stroke
NIH Building 31, Room 8A16
Bethesda, MD 20892
(301) 496-5751

ORGAN TRANSPLANTATION

Children's Transplant Association
P.O. Box 53699
Dallas, TX 75253
(214) 287-8484

Transplant Recipient
International Organization
(TRIO)
244 N. Bellefield Ave.
Pittsburgh, PA 15213
(412) 687-2210

OSTEOPOROSIS

National Osteoporosis
  Foundation
1150 17th St. NW, Suite 500
Washington, DC 20036
(202) 223-2226

OSTOMY

United Ostomy Association
36 Executive Park, Suite 120
Irvine, CA 92714
(714) 660-8624

PAIN

American Chronic Pain
  Association
P.O. Box 850
Rocklin, CA 95677
(916) 632-0922

Chronic Pain Support Group
P.O. Box 148
Penninsula, OH 41264
(216) 526-1530

National Chronic Pain Outreach
  Association
7979 Old Georgetown Road,
  Suite 100
Bethesda, MD 20814-2429
(301) 652-4948

PARALYSIS AND PARAPLEGIA

American Paralysis Association
500 Morris Ave.
Springfield, NJ 07081
(800) 225-0292

In Touch with Kids
National Spinal Cord Injury
  Association
(800) 962-9629
*A network for parents of children with
spinal cord injury or disease.*

National Easter Seal Society
70 E. Lake St.
Chicago, IL 60601
(800) 221-6827
(312) 726-6200

National Spinal Cord Injury
  Association
600 W. Cummings Park, Suite
  2000
Woburn, MA 01801
(800) 962-9629

Paralyzed Veterans of America
801 18th St. NW
Washington, DC 20006
(202) USA-1300

PARKINSON'S DISEASE

National Parkinson's Foundation
1501 NW Ninth Ave.
Miami, FL 33136
(800) 327-4545
(800) 433-7022 in Florida
(800) 400-8448 in California

Parkinson Support Groups of
America
11376 Cherry Hill Road, Suite
204
Beltsville, MD 20705
(301) 937-1545

Parkinson's Disease Foundation
William Black Medical Research
Building
Columbia-Presbyterian Medical
Center
650 W. 168th St.
New York, NY 10032
(800) 457-6676

Parkinson's Educational Program
3900 Birch St., Suite 105
Newport Beach, CA 92660
(800) 344-7872

United Parkinson's Foundation
360 W. Superior St.
Chicago, IL 60610
(312) 664-2344

PHENYLKETONURIA (PKU)

PKU Parents
8 Myrtle Lane
San Anselmo, CA 94960
(415) 457-4632

POLIO

International Polio Network
510 Oakland Ave., Suite 206
St. Louis, MO 63110
(314) 361-0475

Polio Society
P.O. Box 106273
Washington, DC 20016
(301) 897-8180

Post-Polio League for
Information and Outreach
(703) 273-8171

United Post-Polio Survivors
P.O. Box 273
Itasca, IL 60143-0273
(312) 784-6332 voice-only
(800) 526-0844 TDD, in Illinois
only

SCLERODERMA

Scleroderma Federation
Peabody Office Bldg.
One Newbury St.
Peabody, MA 01960
(508) 535-6600

United Scleroderma Foundation,
Inc.
(800) 722-HOPE
In California: (408) 728-2202

SICKLE-CELL ANEMIA

Sickle Cell Community Network
c/o Parents Helping Parents
535 Race St., Suite 120
San Jose, CA 95126
(408) 288-5010

Sickle Cell Disease Association
of America (formerly the
National Association for
Sickle Cell Disease)
3545 Wilshire Blvd., Suite 1106
Los Angeles, CA 90010
(213) 736-5455
(800) 421-8453

Sickle Cell Self-Help
Association
(213) 936-7025

SPINA BIFIDA

Spina Bifida Association of
America
(800) 621-3141
(202) 944-3285

STROKE

American Heart Association
7272 Greenville Ave.
Dallas, TX 75231
(214) 373-6300

Courage Stroke Network
c/o Courage Center
3915 Golden Valley Road
Golden Valley, MN 55422
(800) 553-6321

National Institute of
Neurological Disorders and
Stroke
9000 Rockville Parkway,
Building 31
Room 8A-16
Bethesda, MD 20892
(301) 496-5751

National Stroke Association
300 East Hampden Ave., Suite
240
Englewood, CO 80110-2654
(303) 762-9922
(800) STROKES

Stroke Clubs, International
805 12th St.
Galveston, TX 77550
(409) 762-1022

SUBSTANCE ABUSE

Alcoholics Anonymous World
  Services
(212) 870-3400

Al-Anon Family Group
  Headquarters
(212) 302-7240

Betty Ford Center
3900 Bob Hope Drive
Rancho Mirage, CA 92270
(619) 773-4100

Children of Alcoholics
  Foundation
(212) 754-0656

Cocaine Anonymous World
  Services
(310) 559-5833
(800) 347-8998 *for meeting
  locations*

Do It Now Foundation
(602) 491-0393

Families Anonymous
P.O. Box 528
Van Nuys, CA 91408
(818) 989-7841

National Association for
  Children of Alcoholics
(301) 468-0985

National Council on Alcoholism
  and Drug Dependence
12 West 21st St.
New York, NY 10010
(800) NCA-CALL
(212) 206-6770

Rational Recovery Systems
P.O. Box 800
Lotus, CA 95651
(916) 621-4374

URINARY TRACT

American Foundation for
  Urologic Disease
300 W. Pratt St., Suite 401
Baltimore, MD 21201
(800) 242-2383

Interstitial Cystitis Association
P.O. Box 1553, Madison Square
  Station
New York, NY 10159
(212) 979-6057
(800) HELP-ICA

VISUAL IMPAIRMENT

American Council of the Blind
1155 15th St. NW, Suite 720
Washington, DC 20005
(202) 467-5081
(800) 424-8666

American Foundation for the
  Blind
15 W. 16th St.
New York, NY 10011
(800) AF-BLIND
(212) 620-2000
Ask for "The Directory of Services for the Visually Impaired," a state-by-state listing of services available nationally.

The Associated Blind
135 W. 23rd St.
New York, NY 10011
(212) 255-1122

Associated Services for the Blind
919 Walnut St.
Philadelphia, PA 19107
(215) 627-0600

National Association for Parents
  of the Visually Impaired
2180 Linway
Beloit, WI 53511
(608) 362-4945
(800) 562-6265

OTHER ISSUES

BEREAVEMENT

The Compassionate Friends
P.O. Box 3696
Oakbrook, IL 60522-3696
(708) 990-0010
Support groups and information for bereaved family members. Emphasizes positive resolution to grief.

HOSPITALITY HOUSES FOR FAMILIES OF THOSE UNDERGOING LONG-TERM TREATMENT

National Association of
  Hospitality Houses, Inc.
P.O. Box 8022
Muncie, IN 47304
(800) 542-9730
(317) 288-3226

Ronald McDonald Houses
1 Kroc Drive
Oakbrook, IL 60521
(708) 575-7418

LEGAL PROBLEMS, WILLS, GUARDIANSHIPS, AND TRUSTS

American Bar Association
   Commission on Legal
   Problems of the Elderly
(202) 331-2297

Concern for Dying
(212) 246-6962
For information on living wills.

The Living Bank
(800) 528-2971
For information on organ donation.

National Academy of Elder Law
Attorneys
(602) 881-4005

NUTRITION AND DIET

The American Heart Association
7320 Greenville Ave.
Dallas, TX 75231
For advice on healthful, low-fat diets.

National Center for Nutrition
   and Dietetics
216 W. Jackson Blvd., Suite 800
Chicago, IL 60606-6995
(800) 366-1655

Nutrition Education Association
P.O. Box 20301
3647 Glen Haven
Houston, TX 77225
(713) 665-2946

PRESCRIPTION DRUGS

The American Council for Drug
   Education
204 Monroe St.
Rockville, MD 20850
(800) 488-DRUG

The National Council on Patient
   Education
666 11th St. NW, Suite 810
Washington, DC 20001
(202) 347-6711
Ask for pamphlet on prescriptions.

Appendix C

BOOKS
YOU MAY FIND
HELPFUL

MEDICAL GUIDES

American Medical Association. *The American Medical Association Family Medical Guide*, rev. ed. New York: Random House, 1987.
———. *The American Medical Association Guide to Your Family's Symptoms*. New York: Random House, 1992.
Johns Hopkins Medical Letter, Health Over 50 Editors. *The Johns Hopkins Medical Handbook: The 100 Major Medical Disorders of People Over the Age of 50*. New York: Random House, 1992.
Larson, David E., ed. *The Mayo Clinic Family Health Book*. New York: Morrow, 1991.
Margolis, Simeon, ed. *The Johns Hopkins Handbook of Drugs: Specially Edited and Organized by Disease for People Over 50*. New York: Rebus, 1993.
University of California, Berkeley. *The Wellness Encyclopedia: The Comprehensive Resource to Safeguarding Health and Preventing Illness*. Boston: Houghton Mifflin, 1991.

GENERAL

Bass, Deborah S. *Caring Families: Supports and Interventions.* Silver Spring, MD: National Association of Social Workers, 1990.

Biegel, David E., Esther Sales, and Richard Schulz. *Family Caregiving in Chronic Illness.* Newbury Park, CA: Sage, 1991.

Bloomfield, Harold, and Leonard Felder. *Making Peace with Your Parents.* New York: Ballantine, 1985.

Committee on Handicaps Group for the Advancement of Psychiatry. *Caring for People with Physical Impairment: The Journey Back* (Report #135). Washington, DC: American Psychiatric Press, 1993.

Danskin, David G. *Quicki-Mini Stress Management Strategies for You, a Person with a Disability.* Manhattan, KS: Guild Hall Publications, 1988.

DeGraff, Alfred H. *Home Health Aides: How to Manage the People Who Help You.* Clifton Park, NY: Saratoga Access Publications, 1988.

Dempcy, Mary, and Rene Tilhista. *Stress Personalities: A Look Inside Ourselves.* Bolinas, CA: Focal Point Press, 1991.

Dixon, Barbara M., and Josleen Wilson. *Good Health for African Americans.* New York: Crown, 1994.

Doka, Kenneth J. *Living with Life-Threatening Illness.* New York: Lexington, 1993.

Felder, Leonard. *When a Loved One Is Ill: How to Take Better Care of Your Loved One, Your Family, and Yourself.* New York: Penguin, 1990.

Finston, Peggy. *Parenting Plus: Raising Children with Special Health Needs.* New York: Penguin, 1990.

Freimuth, Vicki S., et al. *Searching for Health Information.* Philadelphia: University of Pennsylvania Press, 1989.

Friedman, Jo-Ann. *Home Health Care: A Complete Guide for Patients and Their Families.* New York: Norton, 1987.

Garee, B., ed. *Ideas for Making Your Home Accessible.* Bloomington, IL: Cheever Publishing, 1979.

Glidden, Laraine Masters. *Parents for Children, Children for Parents: The Adoption Alternative.* Washington, DC: American Association on Mental Retardation, 1989. *(For those considering adopting a child with disabilities.)*

Goldfarb, Lori A., Mary Jane Brotherson, Jean Ann Summers, and Ann
P. Turnbull. *Meeting the Challenge of Disability or Chronic Illness: A Family
Guide.* Baltimore, MD: Paul H. Brookes, 1986.

Gumbrium, Jaber F. *Speaking of Life: Horizons of Meaning for Nursing Home
Residents.* Hawthorne, NY: Aldine De Gruyter, 1993.

Harbaugh, Gary L. *Caring for the Caregiver.* Washington, DC: The Alban
Institute, 1992.

Heath, Angela. *Long Distance Caregiving.* Lakewood, CO: American
Source Books, 1993.

Horne, Jo. *A Survival Guide for Family Caregivers: Strength, Support, and
Sources of Help for All Those Caring for Aging or Impaired Family Members.*
Minneapolis: CompCare, 1991.

Horowitz, Karen E., and Douglas M. Lanes. *Witness to Illness: Strategies
for Caregiving and Coping.* Reading, MA: Addison-Wesley, 1992.

Karr, Katherine L. *Taking Time for Me: How Caregivers Can Effectively Deal
with Stress.* Buffalo: Prometheus Books, 1992.

Kelley, Jerry D., and Lex Frieden. *Go for It: A Book on Sports and Recreation for Persons with Disabilities.* New York: Harcourt Brace Jovanovich, 1989.

Kievman, Beverly, with Susie Blackmun. *For Better or for Worse: A Couple's
Guide to Dealing with Chronic Illness.* Chicago: Contemporary Books,
1989.

Kriegsman, Kay Harris, Elinor I. Zaslow, and Jennifer D'Zmura-
Rechsteiner. *Taking Charge: Teenagers Talk about Life and Physical Disabilities.* Rockville, MD: Woodbine House, 1992.

Lobato, Debra J. *Brothers, Sisters, and Special Needs: Information and Activities
for Helping Young Siblings of Children with Chronic Illnesses and Developmental Disabilities.* Baltimore: Paul H. Brookes, 1990.

McAnaney, Kate Divine. *I Wish . . . Dreams and Realities of Parenting a
Special Needs Child.* Sacramento: United Cerebral Palsy Association of
California, 1992.

Miller, Nancy B. *Nobody's Perfect: Living and Growing with Children Who
Have Special Needs.* Baltimore: Paul H. Brookes, 1994.

Mills, Joyce C. *Little Tree: A Story for Children with Serious Medical Problems.*
New York: Brunner/Mazel, 1992.

Moore, Cory. *A Reader's Guide: For Parents of Children with Mental, Physical, or Emotional Disabilities*, 3rd ed. Rockville, MD: Woodbine House, 1990.

Neidrick, Darla J. *Caring for Your Own: Nursing the Ill at Home.* New York: Wiley, 1988.

Nelson-Morrill, Creston, ed. *Florida Caregivers Handbook*, rev. 2nd ed. Tallahassee, FL: HealthTrac Books, 1993.

Pitzele, Sefra Kobrin. *We Are Not Alone: Learning to Live with Chronic Illness.* New York: Workman, 1986.

Pollin, Irene, and Susan K. Golant. *Taking Charge: Overcoming the Challenges of Long-Term Illness.* New York: Times Books, 1994.

Ransom, Judy Griffith. *The Courage to Care.* Nashville, TN: Upper Room Books, 1994.

Ratto, L. L. *Coping with the Physically Challenged Brother or Sister.* New York: Rosen Publishing Group, 1992.

Royse, Jane, and Sheryl Niebuhr. *Take Care!* St. Paul: Amherst H. Wilder Foundation, 1989.

Sankar, A. *Dying at Home: A Family Guide for Caregiving.* Baltimore: Johns Hopkins University Press, 1991.

Shields, Craig V. *Strategies: A Practical Guide for Dealing with Professionals and Human Service Systems.* Baltimore: Paul H. Brookes, 1987.

Simons, Robin. *After the Tears: Parents Talk About Raising a Child with a Disability.* New York: Harcourt Brace Jovanovich, 1987.

Singer, George H., and Larry K. Irvin, eds. *Support for Caregiving Families: Enabling Positive Adaptation to Disability.* Baltimore: Paul H. Brookes, 1989.

Strong, Maggie. *Mainstay: For the Well Spouse of the Chronically Ill.* New York: Penguin, 1988.

Weiss, Louise. *Access to the World: A Travel Guide for the Handicapped.* New York: Facts on File, 1983.

White, Barbara, and Edward Madara, eds. *The Self-Help Sourcebook: Finding and Forming Mutual Aid Self-Help Groups*, 4th edition. Denville, NJ: American Self-Help Clearinghouse, 1993.

BOOKS FOR SPECIFIC CONDITIONS
(Alphabetical by condition)

AGING

Cadmus, Robert R. *Caring for Your Aging Parents: A Concerned Person's Complete Guide for Children of the Elderly.* Englewood Cliffs, NJ: Prentice-Hall, 1984.

Carlin, Vivian F., and Vivian E. Greenberg. *Should Mom Live with Us? And Is Happiness Possible If She Does?* New York: Lexington/Free Press, 1992.

Cohen, Donna, and Carl Eisdorfer. *Seven Steps to Effective Parent Care: A Planning and Action Guide for Adult Children with Aging Parents.* New York: Putnam, 1993.

Edinberg, Mark. *Talking with Your Aging Parents.* Boston: Shambhala, 1987.

Greenberg, Vivian E. *Your Best Is Good Enough: Aging Parents and Your Emotions.* New York: Lexington, 1989.

Hooyman, Nancy, and Wendy Lustbader. *Taking Care of Your Aging Family Members: A Practical Guide.* New York: Free Press, 1988.

Horne, Jo. *Caregiving: Helping an Aging Loved One.* Glenview, IL: Scott, Foresman and Co., 1985.

Kenny, James, and Stephen Spicer. *Caring for Your Aging Parent: A Practical Guide to the Challenges and Choices.* Cincinnati: St. Anthony Messenger Press, 1984.

Levin, Nora. *How to Care for Your Parents: A Handbook for Adult Children.* Friday Harbor, WA: Storm King Press, 1990.

Norris, Jane, ed. *Daughters of the Elderly: Building Partnerships in Caregiving.* Bloomington: Indiana University Press, 1988.

Rob, Caroline. *The Caregiver's Guide: Helping Elderly Relatives Cope with Health and Safety Problems.* Boston: Houghton Mifflin, 1991.

Silverstone, Barbara, and Helen K. Hyman. *You and Your Aging Parent: The Modern Family's Guide to Emotional, Physical, and Financial Problems.* New York: Pantheon, 1990.

————. *Growing Old Together: A Couples' Guide to Understanding and Coping with the Challenges of Later Life.* New York: Pantheon, 1992.

Trieschmann, Roberta B. *Aging with a Disability.* New York: Demos Publications, 1987.

AIDS

Agency for Health Care Policy and Research. *Evaluation and Management of Early HIV Infection: A Clinician's Guide* (I.D. 604). Washington, DC: U.S. Public Health Service, Department of Health and Human Services, 1994. *(For a free copy, call (800) 342-AIDS.)*

American Red Cross. *A Guide to Home Care for the Person Living with AIDS.* Washington, DC: American Red Cross, 1993.

Alyson, Sasha. *You Can Do Something About AIDS.* Boston: The Stop AIDS Project, 1988.

AmFAR Treatment Information Services. *AmFAR AIDS/HIV Treatment Directory.* New York: American Foundation for AIDS Research. *(Updated and revised every 90 days. Lists clinical trials, treatment developments, locations of studies, etc. Available free from the CDC National AIDS Clearinghouse at (800) 458-5231 or directly from AmFAR at (800) 39-AMFAR.)*

Martelli, Leonard J. *When Someone You Know Has AIDS: A Practical Guide,* rev. ed. New York: Crown, 1993.

Wickwire, Peggy. *Nutrition and HIV: Your Choices Make a Difference.* Nashville, TN: Tennessee Department of Health, 1990. *(One copy available free. Call (615) 741-7500.)*

ALLERGY

American Allergy Association. *Living with Allergies.* Menlo Park, CA: Allergy Publications.

————. *Allergy Products Directory.* Menlo Park, CA: Allergy Publications, 1987.

Feldman, B. Robert, and David Carroll. *Complete Book of Children's Allergies.* New York: Warner, 1989.

ALS (LOU GEHRIG'S DISEASE)

ALS Association. Managing ALS Manuals: *Finding Help. Managing Muscular Weakness. Managing Breathing Problems. Managing Swallowing Problems. Solving Communication Problems.* Woodland Hills, CA: ALS Association, 1987.

Mitsumoto, Hiroshi, and Forbes H. Norris, Jr., eds. *Amyotropic Lateral Sclerosis: A Comprehensive Guide to Management.* New York: Demos Publications, 1994.

Rabin, Roni. *Six Parts Love: One Family's Battle with Lou Gehrig's Disease.* New York: Scribner's, 1985.

ALZHEIMER'S DISEASE

Alzheimer's Association, Patient and Family Services. *Family Guide for Alzheimer Care in Residential Settings.* Chicago: Alzheimer's Association, 1992.

Aronson, Miriam. *Understanding Alzheimer's Disease.* New York: Scribner's, 1988.

Cohen, Donna, and Carl Eisdorfer. *The Loss of Self: A Family Resource for the Care of Alzheimer's Disease and Related Disorders.* New York: New American Library, 1986.

Coughlan, Patricia Brown. *Facing Alzheimer's.* New York: Ballantine, 1993.

Greutzner, Howard. *Alzheimer's: A Caregiver's Guide and Sourcebook.* New York: Wiley, 1992.

Lawson Keller, Judy, ed. *The Male Caregivers' Guidebook: Caring for Your Loved One with Alzheimer's at Home.* Des Moines: Alzheimer's Association, Iowa Golden Chapter, 1992.

Mace, Nancy L., and Peter V. Rabins. *The Thirty-six-Hour Day: A Family Guide to Caring for Persons with Alzheimer's Disease, Related Dementing Illnesses, and Memory Loss in Later Life,* rev. ed. New York: Warner, 1992.

Roberts, D. Jeanne. *Taking Care of Caregivers: For Families and Others Who Care for People with Alzheimer's Disease and Other Forms of Dementia.* Palo Alto, CA: Bull Publishing, 1991.

United States Congress, Office of Technology Assessment. *Special Care Units for People with Alzheimer's and Other Dementias: Consumer Education, Research, Regulatory, and Reimbursement Issues: Summary.* Washington, DC: U.S. Government Printing Office, 1992. GPO stock no.: 052-003-01296-1.

AMPUTATION

Janzen, John M. *Who Is There to Share the Dream? Finding Purpose and Potential After Tragedy.* Saratoga, CA: R & E Publishers, 1988.

ARTHRITIS

Brewer, Earl J., and Kathy C. Angel. *Parenting a Child with Arthritis: A Practical, Empathic Guide to Help You and Your Child Live with Arthritis.* Los Angeles: Lowell House, 1992.

Phillips, Robert H. *Coping with Osteoarthritis: A Guide to Living with Arthritis for You and Your Family.* Garden City, NY: Avery, 1989.

Shen, Harry, and Cheryl Solimini. *Living with Arthritis: Successful Strategies to Help Manage the Pain and Remain Active.* New York: Ballantine, 1993.

ASTHMA

Decker, John L., and Michael A. Kaliner. *Understanding and Managing Asthma.* New York: Avon, 1988.

Plaut, Thomas. *Children with Asthma: A Manual for Parents.* Amherst, MA: Pedipress, 1989.

Rudoff, Carol. *Asthma Resources Directory.* Menlo Park, CA: Allergy Publications, 1990.

AUTISM

Greenfield, Josh. *A Place for Noah.* New York: Holt, 1978.

Harris, Sandra L. *Siblings of Children with Autism.* Rockville, MD: Woodbine House, 1994.

Hart, Charles A. *A Parent's Guide to Autism.* New York: Pocket, 1993.

Powers, Michael D. *Children with Autism: A Parents' Guide.* Rockville, MD: Woodbine House, 1989.

Simpson, Richard L., and Paul Zionts. *Autism: Information and Resources for Parents, Families, and Professionals.* Austin, TX: Pro-Ed, 1992.

Turnbull, Ann P., et al., eds. *Cognitive Coping, Families, and Disabilities.* Baltimore: Paul H. Brookes, 1993.

CANCER

Aker, Saundra, and Polly Lennsen. *A Guide to Good Nutrition During and After Chemotherapy and Radiation,* 3rd ed. Seattle: The Fred Hutchinson Cancer Research Center Clinical Nutrition Program, 1988. (*Can be ordered by calling* (206) 667-4834.)

Altman, Roberta, and Michael J. Sarg. *The Cancer Dictionary.* New York: Facts on File, 1992.

American Cancer Society, California Division. *Caring for the Patient with Cancer at Home: A Guide for Patients and Families* (4656). Atlanta: American Cancer Society, 1990. (*Free pamphlet available by calling* (800) ACS-2345.)

Anderson, Greg. *Fifty Essential Things to Do When the Doctor Says It's Cancer.* New York: NAL-Dutton, 1993.

Benjamin, Harold H. *From Victim to Victor: The Wellness Community Guide to Fighting for Recovery for Cancer Patients and Their Families.* Los Angeles: Jeremy P. Tarcher, 1987.

Bruning, Nancy. *Coping with Chemotherapy.* New York: Ballantine, 1993.

Cox, Barbara G., et al., eds. *Living with Lung Cancer: A Guide for Patients and Their Families,* 3rd ed. Gainesville, FL: Triad Publishing, 1992.

Dodd, Marilyn J. *Managing the Side Effects of Chemotherapy and Radiation.* New York: Prentice-Hall, 1991.

Dollinger, Malin, Ernest H. Rosenbaum, and Greg Cable. *Everyone's Guide to Cancer Therapy: How Cancer Is Diagnosed, Treated, and Managed on a Day-to-Day Basis.* Kansas City, MO: Andrews and McMeel, 1991.

Fabian, Carol. *Recovering from Breast Cancer: A Doctor's Guide for Women and Their Families.* New York: HarperCollins, 1992.

Harpham, Wendy Schlessel. *Diagnosis Cancer: Your Guide Through the First Few Months.* New York: Norton, 1992.

Johnson, F. Leonard, and Ellen L. O'Connell, eds. *The Candlelighters Guide to Bone Marrow Transplants in Children.* Bethesda, MD: The Candlelighters Childhood Cancer Foundation, 1994.

Love, Susan, with Karen Lindsey. *Dr. Susan Love's Breast Book.* Reading, MA: Addison-Wesley, 1990.

Morra, Marion, and Eve Potts. *Choices,* 3rd ed. New York: Avon, 1994.

Mullan, Fitzhugh, Barbara Hoffman, and the editors of Consumer Reports Books. *Charting the Journey: An Almanac of Practical Resources for Cancer Survivors.* Yonkers, NY: Consumer Reports, 1990.

Murcia, Andy, and Bob Stewart. *Man to Man: When the Woman You Love Has Breast Cancer.* New York: St. Martin's, 1989.

National Cancer Institute. *Chemotherapy and You: A Guide to Self-Help During Treatment.* Publication No. 92-1136. Bethesda, MD: National Cancer Institute, 1991. *(Can be obtained free by calling (800) 4-CANCER.)*

—————. *Radiation Therapy and You: A Guide to Self-Help During Treatment.* Publication No. 92-2227. Bethesda, MD: National Cancer Institute, 1992. *(Can be obtained free by calling (800) 4-CANCER.)*

—————. *What Are Clinical Trials All About?* Publication No. 92-2706. Bethesda, MD: National Cancer Institute, 1992. *(Can be obtained free by calling (800) 4-CANCER.)*

Nessim, Susan, and Judith Ellis. *Cancervivie: The Challenge of Life After Cancer.* Boston: Houghton Mifflin, 1991.

Ramstack, Janet, and Ernest H. Rosenbaum. *Nutrition for the Chemotherapy Patient.* Menlo Park, CA: Bull Publishing, 1992.

Rollin, Betty. *First You Cry.* New York: HarperCollins, 1993.

Rosenblum, D. *A Time to Hear, a Time to Help: Listening to People with Cancer.* New York: Free Press, 1993.

Spiegel, David. *Living Beyond Limits.* New York: Times Books, 1993.

Stewart, Susan K. *Bone Marrow Transplants: A Book of Basics for Patients.*

Highland Park, IL: BMT Newsletter, 1992. *(Available from BMT Newsletter, (708) 831-1913.)*

Williams, Wendy. *The Power Within: True Stories of Exceptional Cancer Patients Who Fought Back with Hope.* New York: Simon & Schuster, 1990.

Wilson, Josleen. *The American Society of Plastic and Reconstructive Surgeons Guide to Cosmetic Surgery.* New York: Simon & Schuster, 1992.

Yale Comprehensive Cancer Center and the National Cancer Institute. *Questions and Answers About Pain Control: A Guide for People with Cancer and Their Families* (4518-PS). Atlanta: American Cancer Society, 1992. *(Available from the American Cancer Society, (800) ACS-2345 or the National Cancer Institute, (800) 4-CANCER.)*

CEREBRAL PALSY

Finnie, Nancie R. *Handling the Young Cerebral Palsied Child at Home.* New York: Dutton, 1974.

Geralis, Elaine, ed. *Children with Cerebral Palsy: A Parents' Guide.* Rockville, MD: Woodbine House, 1991.

CHRONIC FATIGUE SYNDROME/EPSTEIN-BARR VIRUS SYNDROME

Bell, David S. *The Disease of a Thousand Names.* Lyndenville, NY: Pollard Publications, 1991.

Berne, Katrina. *Running on Empty: Chronic Immune Dysfunction Syndrome.* Alameda, CA: Hunter House, 1992.

CYSTIC FIBROSIS

Orenstein, David. *Cystic Fibrosis: A Guide for Patient and Family.* New York: Raven, 1989.

DEVELOPMENTAL AND OTHER DISABILITIES

Batshaw, Mark L., and Yvonne M. Perret. *Children with Disabilities: A Medical Primer,* 3rd ed. Baltimore: Paul H. Brookes, 1992.

Cruzie, Kathleen. *Disabled? Yes. Defeated? No.* Englewood Cliffs, NJ: Prentice-Hall, 1982.

Dickman, Irving, and Sol Gordon. *One Miracle at a Time: How to Get Help for Your Disabled Child—From the Experience of Other Parents.* New York: Simon & Schuster, 1985.

Featherstone, Helen. *A Difference in the Family: Living with a Disabled Child.* New York: Penguin, 1981.

Levin, Toby. *Rainbow of Hope: A Guide for the Special Needs Child.* North Miami Beach, FL: Starlight Publishing Co., 1992.

Miezio, Peggy M. *Parenting Children with Disabilities: A Professional Sourcebook for Physicians and Guide for Parents.* New York: Marcel Dekker, 1983.

Nisbet, Jan, ed. *Natural Supports in School, at Work, and in the Community for People with Severe Disabilities.* Baltimore: Paul H. Brookes, 1992.

Pueschel, Sigfried M., James C. Bernier, and Leslie E. Weldenman. *The Special Child: A Source Book for Parents of Children with Developmental Disabilities.* Baltimore: Paul H. Brookes, 1988.

Weiner, Florence. *No Apologies: A Guide to Living with Disabilities, Written by the Real Authorities—People with Disabilities, Their Family and Friends.* New York: St. Martin's, 1986.

DIABETES

American Diabetes Association. *Type II Diabetes: Your Healthy Living Guide.* Alexandria, VA: American Diabetes Association, 1992.

Hornsby, W. Guyton, Jr. ed. *The Fitness Book: For People with Diabetes.* Alexandria, VA: American Diabetes Association, 1994.

Johnson, Robert Wood IV, Sale Johnson, Casey Johnson, and Susan Kleinman. *Managing Your Child's Diabetes.* New York: Maters Media, 1992.

Krall, Leo P., and Richard S. Beaser. *Joslin Diabetes Manual,* 12th ed. Philadelphia: Lea & Febiger, 1989.

Loring, Gloria. *Parenting a Diabetic Child.* Los Angeles: Lowell House/RGA, 1991.

————. *Kids, Food, and Diabetes: A Family Cookbook.* Sherman Oaks, CA: Juvenile Diabetes Foundation, 1991.

Mulder, Linnea. *Sarah and Puffle: A Story for Children About Diabetes.* New York: Brunner/Mazel, 1992.

DIGESTIVE DISORDERS

Banks, Peter A., Daniel H. Present, and Penny Steiner. *The Crohn's Disease and Ulcerative Colitis Fact Book.* New York: Scribner's, 1983.

Brandt, Lawrence J., and Penny Steiner-Grossman. *Treating IBD: A Patient's Guide to Medical and Surgical Management of Inflammatory Bowel Disease.* New York: Raven, 1989.

Steiner-Grossman, Penny, Peter A. Banks, and Daniel H. Present, eds. *People, Not Patients: A Sourcebook for Living with IBD.* New York: National Foundation for Ileitis, 1983.

DOWN SYNDROME

Pueschel, Siegfried M. *A Parent's Guide to Down Syndrome: Toward a Brighter Future.* Baltimore: Paul H. Brookes, 1990.

Stray-Gunderson, Karen. *Babies with Down Syndrome: A New Parents' Guide.* Rockville, MD: Woodbine House, 1986.

Van Dyke, D. C., Phillip Mattheis, Susan Eberly, and Janet Williams, eds. *Medical and Surgical Care for Children with Down Syndrome.* Rockville, MD: Woodbine House, 1994.

EPILEPSY

Freeman, John M., Eileen P. G. Vining, and Diana J. Pillas, eds. *Seizures and Epilepsy in Childhood: A Guide for Parents.* Baltimore: Johns Hopkins University Press, 1990.

Gumnit, Robert J. *Living Well with Epilepsy.* New York: Demos Publications, 1990.

Lechtenberg, Richard. *Epilepsy and the Family.* Cambridge, MA: Harvard University Press, 1984.

Moss, Deborah M. *Lee, the Rabbit with Epilepsy.* Rockville, MD: Woodbine House, 1989.

Reisner, Helen. *Children with Epilepsy: A Parent's Guide.* Rockville, MD: Woodbine House, 1988.

Silverstein, Alvin, and Virginia B. Silverstein. *Epilepsy.* New York: HarperCollins Children's Books, 1990. *(For children 10–15.)*

GENETIC DISEASES

Borfitz, Jeanne M., and Meredith Margolis. *The Home Care Book: A Parents' Guide to Caring for Children with Progressive Neurological Diseases.* Brookline, MA: National Tay-Sachs and Allied Diseases Association, 1994.

HEADACHE

Diamond, Seymour, and Amy Diamond-Vye. *Hope for Your Headache Problem,* rev. ed. Madison, CT: International Universities Press, 1988.

Diamond, Seymour, Diane Francis, and Amy Diamond-Vye. *Headache and Diet: Tyramine-Free Recipes.* Madison, CT: International Universities Press, 1990.

Sacks, Oliver. *Migraine,* rev. ed. Berkeley: University of California Press, 1992.

HEAD INJURY AND COMA

Doman, Glenn. *In a Word: Answers to 1001 Questions Parents Ask About Their Brain-Injured Children.* New York: Doubleday, 1987.

LeWinn, Edward B. *Coma Arousal: The Family as a Team.* Garden City, NY: Doubleday, 1985.

Williams, Janet M., and Thomas Kay, eds. *Head Injury: A Family Matter.* Baltimore: Paul H. Brookes, 1991.

HEARING IMPAIRMENT

Schwartz, Sue, ed. *Choices in Deafness: A Parents' Guide.* Rockville, MD: Woodbine House, 1987.

HEART DISEASE

American Medical Association. *The Straight-Talk No-Nonsense Guide to Heartcare,* rev. ed. New York: Random House, 1984.
American Heart Association Cookbook, Fifth Edition. New York: Times Books, 1991.
Levin, Rhoda. *Heartmates: A Survival Guide for the Cardiac Spouse.* New York: Pocket, 1990.
Ornish, Dean. *Dr. Dean Ornish's Program for Reversing Heart Disease.* New York: Ballantine, 1991.
Schoenberg, Jane, and JoAnn Stichman. *Heart Family Handbook: A Complete Guide for the Entire Family of Anyone with Any Heart Condition—To Help Make It the Speediest, Most Complete Recovery Possible.* Philadelphia: Hanley & Belfus, 1990.
Winston, Mary, ed. *The American Heart Association Kids Cookbook.* New York: Times Books, 1993.
Wolinsky, Harvey, and Gary Furgusun. *The Heart Attack Recovery Handbook.* New York: Warner, 1988.

LUPUS

Aladjem, Henrietta. *Understanding Lupus: What It Is, How to Treat It, How to Cope with It.* New York: Scribner's, 1985.

MENTAL ILLNESS

Alliance for the Mentally Ill. *Mental Illness: A Handbook for Families.* Quebec, Canada: Alliance for the Mentally Ill, Agency for Reintegration into the Community, Project ARC, 1992.
Bernheim, Kayla. *The Caring Family: Living with Chronic Mental Illness.* New York: Random House, 1982.

Chamberlin, Judy. *On Our Own: Patient-Controlled Alternatives to the Mental Health System.* New York: McGraw-Hill, 1978.

Duke, Patty, and Gloria Hockman. *A Brilliant Madness: Living with Manic Depressive Illness.* New York: Bantam, 1992.

Esser, Aristide H., and Sylvia D. Lacey. *Mental Illness: A Homecare Guide.* New York: John Wiley, 1989.

Hatfield, Agnes B. *Coping with Mental Illness in the Family: A Family Guide.* Arlington, VA: National Alliance for the Mentally Ill.

Kerns, Lawrence, and Adrienne Lieberman. *Helping Your Depressed Child: A Reassuring Guide to the Causes and Treatment of Childhood and Adolescent Depression.* Roseville, CA: Prima Publishing, 1993.

Klein, Donald, and Paul Wender. *Understanding Depression: A Complete Guide to Its Diagnosis, Course, and Treatment.* New York: Oxford University Press, 1993.

Laskin, P., and A. Moskowitz. *Wish Upon a Star: A Story for Children with a Parent Who Is Mentally Ill.* New York: Brunner/Mazel, 1991.

McElroy, Evelyn, ed. *Children and Adolescents with Mental Illness: A Parents' Guide.* Rockville, MD: Woodbine House, 1988.

Moorman, Margaret. *My Sister's Keeper: Learning to Cope with a Sibling's Mental Illness.* New York: Viking Penguin, 1993.

Neuman, Frederic. *Caring: Home Treatment for the Emotionally Disturbed.* New York: Dial, 1980.

Papolos, Demitri, and Janice Papolos. *Overcoming Depression*, rev. ed. New York: HarperCollins, 1992.

Rapoport, Judith. *The Boy Who Couldn't Stop Washing: The Experience and Treatment of Obsessive-Compulsive Disorder.* New York: NAL-Dutton, 1990.

Ross, Jerilyn. *Triumph over Fear: A Book of Help and Hope for People with Anxiety, Panic Attacks, and Phobias.* New York: Bantam, 1994.

Torrey, E. Fuller. *Surviving Schizophrenia: A Family Manual.* New York: Harper & Row, 1983.

Woolis, Rebecca. *When Someone You Love Has a Mental Illness: A Handbook for Family, Friends, and Caregivers.* Los Angeles: Jeremy P. Tarcher, 1992.

Yudofsky, Stuart C., and Tom Furguson. *What You Need to Know About Psychiatric Medications.* New York: Grove-Atlantic, 1991.

MENTAL RETARDATION

Baker, Bruce, Stephen Anderson, and Stephen Ambrose. *Parent Training and Developmental Disabilities.* Washington, DC: American Association on Mental Retardation, 1989.

Borthwick-Duffy, Sharon, Keith Wiedman, Todd Little, and Richard Eyman. *Foster Family Care for Persons with Mental Retardation.* Washington, DC: American Association on Mental Retardation, 1993.

Bradley, Valerie, James Knoll, and John Agosta. *Emerging Issues in Family Support.* Washington, DC: American Association on Mental Retardation, 1993.

Kaufman, Sandra Z. *Retarded Isn't Stupid, Mom!* Baltimore: Paul H. Brookes, 1988.

Perske, Robert. *Hope for the Families: New Directions for Parents of Persons with Retardation or Other Disabilities.* Nashville, TN: Abingdon, 1981.

MULTIPLE SCLEROSIS

Carroll, David. *Living with MS.* New York: HarperCollins, 1993.

Kalb, Rosalind C., and Scheinberg, Labe. *Multiple Sclerosis and the Family.* New York: Demos Publications, 1992.

Lechtenberg, Richard. *Multiple Sclerosis Fact Book.* Philadelphia: F. A. Davis, 1988.

Shuman, Robert, and Janice Schwartz. *Understanding Multiple Sclerosis: A Guidebook for Families.* New York: Scribner's, 1988.

Strong, Maggie. *Mainstay: For the Well Spouse of the Chronically Ill.* New York: Penguin, 1988.

Wolf, John K. *Mastering Multiple Sclerosis: A Guide to Management,* 2nd ed. Rutland, VA: Academy Books, 1987.

NEUROMUSCULAR DISORDERS
(Muscular Dystrophy, ALS, Myasthenia Gravis, Charcot-Marie-Tooth Syndrome)

Ringel, Steven P. *Neuromuscular Disorders: A Guide for Patient and Family.* New York: Raven, 1987.

ORGAN TRANSPLANTATION

Maier, Frank. *Sweet Reprieve.* New York: Crown, 1991.
Starzl, Thomas E. *The Puzzle People: Memoirs of a Transplant Surgeon.* Pittsburgh: University of Pittsburgh Press, 1992.
Terasaki, Paul A., and Jane Schoenberg, eds. *Transplant Success Stories 1993: The True Triumph of Transplantation.* Los Angeles: The Regents of the University of California, UCLA Tissue Typing Lab, 1993.

OSTEOPOROSIS

National Osteoporosis Foundation and the Osteoporosis Center, University of Connecticut Health Center. *Boning Up on Osteoporosis: A Guide to Prevention and Treatment.* Washington, DC: National Osteoporosis Foundation, 1991. *(Available for $3.00 from the National Osteoporosis Foundation at (202) 223-2226.)*

OSTOMY

Mullen, Barbara Dorr, and Kerry Anne McGinn. *The Ostomy Book.* Palo Alto, CA: Bull Publishing, 1992.
Phillips, Robert H. *Coping with an Ostomy.* Wayne, NJ: Avery Publishing, 1986.

PAIN, CHRONIC

American Chronic Pain Association. *ACPA Workbook Manual.* Rocklin, CA: American Chronic Pain Association, 1987. *(Available by writing to ACPA at P.O. Box 850, Rocklin, CA 95677, or call (916) 632-0922.)*

———. *Staying Well: Advanced Pain Management for ACPA Members.* Rocklin, CA: American Chronic Pain Association, 1994. *(Available by writing to ACPA at P.O. Box 850, Rocklin, CA 95677, or call (916) 632-0922.)*

PARALYSIS AND PARAPLEGIA

Ford, Jack R., and Bridget Duckworth. *Physical Management for the Quadriplegic Patient,* 2nd ed. Philadelphia: F. A. Davis, 1987.

Phillips, Lynn. *Spinal Cord Injury: A Guide for Patients and Family.* New York: Raven, 1985.

PARKINSON'S DISEASE

Atwood, Glenna W. *Living Well with Parkinson's.* New York: Wiley, 1991.

Dippel, Raye L., and Thomas J. Hutton, eds. *Caring for the Parkinson's Patient: A Care-Giver Guide.* Buffalo, NY: Prometheus, 1989.

Dorros, Sid, and Donna Dorros. *Parkinson's: A Patient's View.* Arlington, VA: Seven Locks, 1989.

POLIO

Garee, Betty. *Post Polio.* Bloomington, IL: Cheever Publishing, 1987.

SICKLE-CELL ANEMIA

Alta Bates Medical Center. *Mastering Sickle Cell Disease: No One Says It's Easy.* Berkeley: The Adult Sickle Cell Program, Alta Bates Medical Center, 1990. *(Order by phone (510) 204-1609; $3.50.)*

Lessing, Shellye, Elliott Vichinstky, and the State of California Health Services Department, eds. *A Parent's Handbook for Sickle Cell Disease.* Sacramento, CA: State of California, 1993. *(Available free from the National Maternal and Child Health Clearinghouse, 8201 Greensboro Dr., Suite 600, McLean, VA 22102, or call (703) 821-8955.)*

Sickle Cell Disease Association of America. *How to Help Your Child to*

Take It in Stride. Los Angeles, CA: Sickle Cell Disease Association of America.

Spina Bifida

Williamson, G. Gordon. *Children with Spina Bifida: Early Intervention and Preschool Programming.* Baltimore: Paul H. Brookes, 1987.

Stroke

Ahn, Jung. *Recovering from Stroke.* New York: HarperCollins, 1992.

American Heart Association Guide to Stroke. New York: Times Books, 1994.

Ancowitz, Arthur. *The Stroke Book: One-on-One Advice About Stroke Prevention, Management, and Rehabilitation.* New York: Morrow, 1993.

Sarno, John, and Martha Taylor Sarno. *Stroke: A Guide for Patients and Their Families.* New York: McGraw-Hill, 1979.

Schumacher, Nancy, ed. *The Road Ahead: A Stroke Recovery Guide.* New York: Demos Publications, 1987.

Shimberg, Elaine F. *What Stroke Families Should Know.* New York: Ballantine, 1990.

Urinary Tract

Chalker, Rebecca, and Kristene Whitmore. *Overcoming Bladder Disorders.* New York: HarperCollins, 1991.

Visual Impairment

Holbrook, M. Kay. *Children with Visual Impairments: A Parents' Guide.* Rockville, MD: Woodbine House, 1994.

Nousanen, Diane, and Lee Robinson. *Take Charge: A Guide to Resources for Parents of the Visually Impaired.* Watertown, MA: National Association for Parents of the Visually Impaired, 1990.

SPIRITUAL APPROACHES TO ILLNESS AND DEATH

Benson, Herbert. *The Relaxation Response.* New York: Avon, 1976.

Borysenko, Joan. *Minding the Body, Mending the Mind.* New York: Bantam, 1987.

Cousins, Norman. *Anatomy of an Illness as Perceived by the Patient.* New York: Bantam, 1981.

―――. *Head First: The Biology of Hope.* New York: Dutton, 1989.

Frankl, Viktor. *Man's Search for Meaning.* New York: Pocket, 1985.

Kübler-Ross, Elisabeth. *On Death and Dying.* New York: Macmillan, 1969.

Kushner, Harold. *When Bad Things Happen to Good People.* New York: Avon, 1981.

Levine, Stephen. *Who Dies? An Investigation of Conscious Living and Conscious Dying.* Garden City, NY: Anchor/Doubleday, 1987.

Siegel, Bernie. *Love, Medicine, and Miracles.* New York: HarperCollins, 1990.

―――. *Peace, Love, and Healing.* New York: HarperCollins, 1990.

Simonton, Carl O., and Stephanie Simonton. *Getting Well Again.* New York: Bantam, 1980.

Venings, Robert. *A Gift of Hope: How We Survive Our Tragedies.* New York: Ballantine, 1985.

Viorst, Judith. *Necessary Losses.* New York: Fawcett, 1987.

LEGAL AND FINANCIAL ISSUES

American Cancer Society. *Cancer: Your Job, Insurance, and the Law* (4585-PS, 1987). Atlanta: The American Cancer Society, 1987. *(Can be obtained free by calling (800) ACS-2345.)*

The Americans with Disabilities Act: A Guide for People with Disabilities, Their Families and Advocates. *(Available from PACER Center, 4826 Chicago Ave. S., Minneapolis, MN 55417-1055, or call (612) 827-2966.)*

Goldman, Charles D. *Disability Rights Guide: Practical Solutions to Problems*

Affecting People with Disabilities, 2nd ed. Lincoln, NE: Media Publishing, 1990.

Health Insurance Association of America. *The Consumer's Guide to Disability Insurance* (#C104, 1991). Washington, DC: Health Insurance Association of America, 1991. *(Can be obtained free by calling* (202) 223-7708.*)*

———. *The Consumer's Guide to Health Insurance* (#C103, 1991). Washington, DC: Health Insurance Association of America, 1991. *(Can be obtained free by calling* (202) 223-7708.*)*

———. *The Consumer's Guide to Long-Term Care Insurance* (#C101, 1991). Washington, DC: Health Insurance Association of America, 1991. *(Can be obtained free by calling* (202) 223-7708.*)*

———. *The Consumer's Guide to Medicare Supplement Insurance* (#C102, 1991). Washington, DC: Health Insurance Association of America, 1991. *(Can be obtained free by calling* (202) 223-7708.*)*

Mendelsohn, Steven B. *Tax Options and Strategies for People with Disabilities.* New York: Demos Publications, 1993.

Russell, Mark L. *Planning for the Future: Providing a Meaningful Life for a Child with Disability After Your Death.* Evanston, IL: American Publishing, 1993.

Silver, Don. *A Parent's Guide to Wills and Trusts.* Los Angeles: Adams-Hall, 1992.

Smith, Douglas M. *Disability Workbook for Social Security Applicants.* Arnold, MD: Physicians' Disability Services, 1990.

Turnbull, H. Rutherford, III. *Disability and the Family: A Guide to Decisions for Adulthood.* Baltimore: Paul H. Brookes, 1989.

REFERENCES

AARP and The Travelers Companies Foundation. *National Survey of Caregivers: Summary of Findings.* Washington DC: American Association of Retired Persons, 1988.

Altholz, Judith A. S. "Caregiving: The Emotional Rewards and Challenges," in Creston Nelson-Morrill, ed., *Florida Caregivers Handbook,* rev. 2nd ed. Tallahassee, FL: HealthTrac Books, 1993.

Bass, Deborah S. *Caring Families: Supports and Interventions.* Silver Spring, MD: National Association of Social Workers, 1990.

Benjamin, Harold H. *From Victim to Victor.* Los Angeles: Jeremy P. Tarcher, 1987.

Biegel, David E., and Arthur Blum, eds. *Aging and Caregiving: Theory, Research, and Policy.* Newbury Park, CA: Sage, 1990.

Biegel, David E., Esther Sales, and Richard Schulz. *Family Caregiving in Chronic Illness.* Newbury Park, CA: Sage, 1991.

Bowen, Sissy. "Thoughts from Your Editor," *The Middle Flint Area Alzheimer's Caregiver's Companion,* Vol. II, No. 5 September/October, 1993, p. 2.

Carter, Jimmy, and Rosalynn Carter. *Everything to Gain: Making the Most of the Rest of Your Life*. New York: Random House, 1987.

Cody, Pamela. "The Nursing Home Decision," in Creston Nelson-Morrill, ed., *Florida Caregivers Handbook*, rev. 2nd ed. Tallahassee, FL: HealthTrac Books, 1993.

Committee on Handicaps Group for the Advancement of Psychiatry. *Caring for People with Physical Impairment: The Journey Back* (Report #135). Washington, DC: American Psychiatric Press, 1993.

Deets, Horace. "Caregiving Is a Family Issue," *The Rosalynn Carter Institute Newsletter*, Fall/Winter 1993, p. 3.

Edwards, Richard L. "Professional and Family Caregivers: A Social Work Perspective," in Jack A. Nottingham and Joanne Nottingham, eds., *The Professional and Family Caregiver—Dilemmas, Rewards and New Directions*. Americus, GA: The Rosalynn Carter Institute for Human Development, Georgia Southwestern College, 1990.

Felder, Leonard. *When a Loved One Is Ill: How to Take Better Care of Your Loved One, Your Family, and Yourself*. New York: Penguin, 1990.

Ferris, Patricia A., and Catherine A. Marshall. "A Model Project for Families of the Chronically Mentally Ill," *Social Work*, March–April, 1987, p. 110.

Freudenberger, Herbert J. "Recognizing and Dealing with Burnout," in Jack A. Nottingham and Joanne Nottingham, eds., *The Professional and Family Caregiver—Dilemmas, Rewards and New Directions*. Americus, GA: The Rosalynn Carter Institute for Human Development, Georgia Southwestern College, 1990.

Goldfarb, Lori A., Mary Jane Brotherson, Jean Ann Summers, and Ann P. Turnbull. *Meeting the Challenge of Disability or Chronic Illness: A Family Guide*. Baltimore: Paul H. Brookes, 1986.

Goleman, Daniel. "All Too Often, the Doctor Isn't Listening, Studies Show," *New York Times*, November 13, 1991.

Gray, D. Patricia. "The Challenge of Caring for the Chronically Mentally Ill," in Jack A. Nottingham and Joanne Nottingham, eds., *The Professional and Family Caregiver—Dilemmas, Rewards and New Directions*.

Americus, GA: The Rosalynn Carter Institute for Human Development, Georgia Southwestern College, 1990.

Harbaugh, Gary L. *Caring for the Caregiver.* Washington, DC: The Alban Institute, 1992.

Henning, Laura M. "For Better or Worse, in Sickness . . ." *Health Horizons* supplement to *Los Angeles Times*, October 25, 1993, p. 5.

Hunt, Tann. "Legal Aspects of Caregiving," in Creston Nelson-Morrill, ed., *Florida Caregivers Handbook*, rev. 2nd ed. Tallahassee, FL: HealthTrac Books, 1993.

Katz, Alfred H., Hannah L. Hedrick, Daryl Isenberg, et al., eds. *Self-Help: Concepts and Applications*. Philadelphia: Charles Press, 1992.

Kaye, L. W., and J. S. Applegate. "Men as Elder Caregivers: A Response to Changing Families," *American Journal of Orthopsychiatry*, 1990:60, p. 86.

Keitel, Merle A., Stanley H. Cramer, and Michael Zevon. "Spouses of Cancer Patients: A Review of the Literature," *Journal of Counseling and Development*, 1990:69, p. 163.

Keller, M. Jean. "The Role of Leisure Education with Family Caregivers," *Leisure Today/JOPERD*, October 1992, p. 23.

Kosbert, Jordan I. *Family Care of the Elderly*. Newbury Park, CA: Sage, 1992.

Kutner, Lawrence. "Growing Up with a Disabled Sibling Needn't Be Damaging," *New York Times*, December 30, 1993.

Landsman, Ron M. "What If I Die? A Planning Guide for Caregivers," *Take Care!*, Winter 1993:2, p. 1.

Lewin, Tamar. "Keeping Elderly at Home and Care Affordable," *New York Times*, February 14, 1994, p. A1.

Lindgren, Carolyn L. "The Caregiver Career," *IMAGE: Journal of Nursing Scholarship*, 1993:25, p. 214.

Maslach, C., and S. E. Jackson. "The Measurement of Experienced Burnout," *Journal of Occupational Behavior*, 1981:2, p. 99.

Mayeroff, Milton. *On Caring*. New York: HarperCollins, 1990.

Mintz, Suzanne. "Making Decisions in Times of Crisis," *Take Care!* Summer 1993:2, p. 1.

National Family Caregivers Association. "A Support Group Guide: Questions, Answers, and Explanations," *Take Care!* Summer 1993:2, p. 5.

————. "A Guide to Improving Doctor/Caregiver Relationships," *Take Care!* Fall 1993:2, p. 1.

Nelson-Morrill, Creston, ed., *Florida Caregivers Handbook,* rev. 2nd ed. Tallahassee, FL: HealthTrac Books, 1993.

Nottingham, Jack A., and Joanne Nottingham. *The Professional and Family Caregiver—Dilemmas, Rewards and New Directions.* Americus, GA: The Rosalynn Carter Institute for Human Development, Georgia Southwestern College, 1990.

Nottingham, Jack A., David Haigler, David L. Smith, and Pam Davis. *Characteristics, Concerns and Concrete Needs of Formal and Informal Caregivers: Understanding and Appreciating Their Marathon Existence.* Americus, GA: The Rosalynn Carter Institute for Human Development, Georgia Southwestern College, 1993.

Perske, Robert. *Hope for the Families: New Directions for Parents of Persons with Retardation or Other Disabilities.* Nashville, TN: Abingdon, 1981.

Pollin, Irene, and Susan K. Golant. *Taking Charge: Overcoming the Challenges of Long-Term Illness.* New York: Times Books, 1994.

Ring, Karen. "Caring and Grieving," in Creston Nelson-Morrill, ed., *Florida Caregivers Handbook,* rev. 2nd ed. Tallahassee, FL: HealthTrac Books, 1993.

Salisbury, Christine L., and James Intagliata, eds. *Respite Care: Support for Persons with Developmental Disabilities and Their Families.* Baltimore: Paul H. Brookes, 1986.

Shellenbarger, Sue. "The Aging of America Is Making 'Elder Care' a Big Workplace Issue," *Wall Street Journal,* February 16, 1994, p. A1.

Shields, Craig V. *Strategies: A Practical Guide for Dealing with Professionals and Human Service Systems.* Baltimore: Paul H. Brookes, 1987.

Smith, Gregory C., Mary F. Smith, and Ronald W. Toseland. "Problems Identified by Family Caregivers in Counseling," *The Gerontologist,* 1991:31, p. 15.

Strong, Maggie. *Mainstay: For the Well Spouse of the Chronically Ill.* New York: Penguin, 1988.

United States Congress. *Exploding the Myths: Caregiving in America.* Washington, DC: Select Committee on Aging, House of Representatives, Comm. Pub. No. 100-665, Government Printing Office, 1988.

Weber, Ruth E. "Senior Citizen Caregivers: The Experience of Caring for an Aged Family Member," in Jack A. Nottingham and Joanne Nottingham, eds., *The Professional and Family Caregiver—Dilemmas, Rewards and New Directions.* Americus, GA: The Rosalynn Carter Institute for Human Development, Georgia Southwestern College, 1990.

INDEX

Index

lawyers, 62, 64, 65, 66, 67
legal issues:
  books on, 263–64
  organizations for, 242
leisure time and relaxation, 29, 46–47,
    85, 143, 145
leukemia, 232
life expectancy, 33
life insurance, 61, 65–66
life-sustaining technologies, 63–64
  living wills and, 62–63, 64, 65, 242
liver disease, 233
living trusts, 65
living wills, 62–63, 64, 65
  organizations for, 242
loneliness, *see* isolation and loneliness
Lou Gehrig's disease (amyotropic
    lateral sclerosis; ALS):
  books on, 249, 260
  organizations for, 224–25
lung diseases:
  information clearinghouses for, 216
  organizations for, 231, 233
lupus erythematosus:
  books on, 257
  organizations for, 233

Mainstay (Strong), 92–93, 115
marriage, *see* spouse, caring for
Mayeroff, Milton, 7, 8, 10
Mead, Margaret, 14
Medicaid, 181, 189
medical guides, 243
Medicare, 181, 189
  hotline for, 217
medications, prescription, 163
  organization for, 242
meditation, 85, 143
mental health:
  caregiving and, 24, 26–27, 28–30,
    36–37
  information clearinghouses for, 216
  organizations for, 234–35
  Rosalynn Carter's career in, 23–28,
    29–30, 36
mental illness, 4, 6, 24–25, 26, 28, 29,
    33, 35, 40
  books on, 257–59
  organization for, 234
mental retardation:
  books on, 259
  organizations for, 235–36
Mintz, Suzanne G., 116, 201–2
Mitchell, Rosemarie, 113–14, 203–5

Montgomery, Rhonda J. V., 146–48
multiple sclerosis:
  books on, 259
  organizations for, 236
muscular dystrophy, 260
  organization for, 236
musculoskeletal diseases, information
    clearinghouses for, 214
myasthenia gravis, 260

Nakamura, Rose, 126–27
National Family Caregivers
    Association, 116, 117, 164, 202
National Federation of Interfaith
    Volunteer Caregivers, Inc., 35,
    123, 125–29, 142
National Quality Caregiving Coalition
    (NQCC), 40
neurological disorders, 236, 239
neuromuscular disorders, resources on,
    260
  ALS, 224–25, 249, 260
  muscular dystrophy, 236, 260
Nottingham, Jack, 34, 42–43
nurses, 58, 95, 97, 142, 145
  at nursing homes, 184
nursing homes, 12, 57, 61, 173, 175–
    76, 177, 178–79, 181–82
  conditions at, 187–88
  emotional climate at, 188
  family councils at, 187
  financial arrangements with, 189
  food at, 186–87
  levels of care in, 182–83
  licensing and rating of, 184
  practical details and, 188–89
  professional caregivers' views on,
    190
  quality and stability of staff at,
    184–85
  role of family and friends in, 193–
    94
  sense of loss and, 191–93
  services and activities available at,
    185–86
  social workers at, 187
  what to look for in, 183–89
  see also institutions,
    institutionalization
nutrition, 242

obsessive compulsive disorder, 235
On Caring (Mayeroff), 7, 8, 10
organ donation, 242